Heralds of God

Heralds of God

Homilies for
Saints' & Holy Days

Herbert O'Driscoll

Anglican Book Centre
Toronto, Canada

1995
Anglican Book Centre
600 Jarvis Street
Toronto, Ontario
M4Y 2J6 Canada

Canadian Cataloging in Publication Data:
O'Driscoll, Herbert, 1928–
  Heralds of God

ISBN 1–55126–115–4

1. Christian saints – Prayer-books and devotions –
English. 2. Fasts and feasts – Prayer-books and
devotions – English. 3. Christian saints –
Meditations. 4. Collects – Meditations.
5. Anglican Church of Canada. Book of Common Prayer –
Meditations. I. Title.

BV30.047 1995 242'.3 C95-930873-3

Contents

for mother,
who, in her 94th year,
will read these pages in between
knitting industriously, walking smartly,
baking deliciously, travelling hopefully,
and worshipping faithfully.

Preface

It seems to me that we go on recalling the men and women we call saints because they do something for us. They model ways of being Christian, and the greatest of them do this in ways that speak to us across time and change and circumstance.

In the prayer books that enshrine our Christian traditions, we have a small number of them, all from the opening years of the Christian story. Together they form the earliest group portrait of our Christian family. To meet them is to meet elements of ourselves.

In these pages I have attempted to arrange such meetings. I have asked you to suspend belief while I imagine what it might be like to encounter a figure of the New Testament as a kind of time traveller, able to meet us in our time and to respond to our curiosity about his or her experience and world.

Naturally there are things we can never know. One can probe the riches of the tradition; one cannot or should not re-invent it. We need to be reminded that those who lived, and often died, for Jesus Christ were human beings very much like us, coping, as we have to cope, with the subtle and complex challenges of life. If I have in any way achieved this, I shall be happy with these pages.

I want to say thank you to certain people, especially to Cynthia Shattuck of Cowley Press who edited my original manuscript for the U.S.A. edition, shaping my early text into what you have in your hands. Thank you also to Robert Maclennan whose interest and additional work shaped this Canadian edition. Incidentally, be aware that the U.S.A. edition of this work bears the title *For all the Saints*.

Thank you's tend to multiply if only because they are many in the writing of any book. A special thanks to my wife, Paula, whose almost infinite capacity for living with a husband closeted with a word processor makes her, in her own way, a rather special and much-loved kind of saint.

As you read these pages, taking time from your own probably frantic pursuit of some semblance of contemporary saintliness, I hope that they will communicate something of the quality of these men and women who pursued the same quest before us, tasting as we do its joys and sorrows, successes and failures.

Victoria, B.C.
Lent 1995

The
Holy Innocents

Almighty God, our heavenly Father,
whose children suffered at the hands of Herod,
receive, we pray, all innocent victims
into the arms of your mercy.
By your great might frustrate all evil designs
and establish your reign of justice, love, and peace;
through Jesus Christ our Lord,
who lives and reigns with you and the Holy Spirit,
one God, now and for ever.

Jeremiah 31.15-17 or Revelation 21.1-7
Psalm 124
Matthew 2.13-18

℞

The taxi swings in a wide arc that scatters dust and stones as it comes to halt. When we step out into the brutal heat of the July sun the warmth comes up from the bone-dry ground in waves, almost physically hitting my face. The driver points to the north, toward the huge unpaved ramp; he says simply, "Up there." We pay him and begin the climb, first reaching for the ever-present water bottle and drinking deeply. Twice more before we reach the top we will rest and drink and look about us as the elevation offers us a spreading panorama.

Over to the west, only about eight kilometers or so, Bethlehem spreads across the ridge that runs north and south, while further to the north the suburbs of Jerusalem creep southward. That alone would have made Herod edgy. He liked to keep his distance from centers of population, and with good reason. He built this extraordinary fortress on top of a man-made mountain to ensure that no enemy—and he had many—could get to him.

Near the summit, while I gulp down what is left of the lukewarm water, I look back down the ramp and see them in my imagination. There would have been more than three. Magi were significant power-brokers in the Persian empire and they would not have traveled without their comforts. That meant servants, at least one or two each, men who could wield a sword if necessary on the long, dangerous journey. I watch them as they come toward me. Separated by two millennia of time, we meet on this endless sloping mountain road.

They pass on beyond me, moving slowly and carefully up toward the point where the great, heavily-guarded entrance once stood. They know they are entering a situation fraught with suspicion and paranoia, where sudden movements or large retinues could be misinterpreted.

Their host, Herod, is in his mid-seventies, desperately ill, deeply threatened, but still extremely dangerous. The single question of the visitor from Persia has set every nerve-end throbbing in the old dictator. The soft, cultured voice of the visitor merely asks, "Where is he that is born king of the Jews?" It is a tribute to Herod's self-control that there is no explosion at hearing of the birth of another king within a few miles of his fortress palace. The iron rules of Middle Eastern hospitality dictate that everything must proceed with utmost pleasantness and good fellowship, so Herod says nothing apart from the deliberately casual request that if the guests find the child, they might consider letting their host know. The guests, themselves subtle diplomats, are not for a moment deceived by the mildness of his reply.

After a night's sleep the great doors of the Herodium open for their leaving, closing again behind them, and they begin the long, slow descent around the curve of the hill. Within a mile of the palace they have already agreed among themselves that they have no intention of coming back. They scent danger on the wind even before they get to the village on the hill a few miles in front of them to the west. They know the child is somewhere along the ridge, waiting for them in his mother's arms.

The three visitors had barely presented their exotic gifts to the baby and departed when another guest arrived at the crude door. We will never know who this visitor was, whether it was a neighbor, whether a man or a woman. All we know is that it was an angel in disguise, because the quick visit with its warning made the difference between life and death. Even as the orders were being bellowed out in the Herodium guardroom and stables, as the horses were being saddled and the short, stabbing swords were being pushed into scabbards, the family was heading south toward Gaza and the desert. When the death squad came to Bethlehem it carried out the king's orders. Children under two years, so the orders said, and like good soldiers they followed orders.

Even in the late twentieth century we are used to such orders and to such death squads. We who claim the child of Bethlehem as Lord have supported regimes that have carried out Herod's work in a hundred Bethlehems. We have slaughtered children two years and under from the clinical distance of twenty thousand feet in the sky, and wiped out the lives of many more by our casual signing of a trade policy here, a withdrawal of troops there, a casual taxing of a Third World product from some corner of the globe we could not even find on a map. We can point to a score of Bethlehems with names like Sarajevo and Rwanda; we do not even have to go outside our own country to find Bethlehems.

At least Herod was acting within the laws and assumptions of the Roman empire, where children lived or died at the pleasure of the state until they were three years old. Not very many years after Herod's decree, and for much the same kind of imagined threat to his power, the emperor Nero ordered a similar pogrom among the newborn children of prominent Roman families.

In speaking of such things, in going far beyond the Bethlehem of long ago, we are only following the later lines of the collect of this day. It too goes from the specific to the numberless tragedies hidden in the three words "all innocent victims." There is an irony in the next words as we pray that "all evil designs" may be frustrated. We seem to be implying that it is only under such regimes that pogroms of this kind occur, but tragedy also arises from the designs of well-intentioned men and women, all of whom are good and decent and well-meaning.

At this point the collect takes us out on to the widest stage of all. "Establish," we ask of God, "your reign of justice, love, and peace." Within minutes of making this petition, we will hear as part of the Liturgy of the Word the great cosmic vision of John from Revelation: the city that we are utterly incapable of building here on earth, the holy city where justice, love, and peace are finally accessible.

Why read of something so vast and cosmic on this day of Holy Innocents? Because we know all too well that our best decisions, our most carefully worked-out policies, our most well-intentioned programs will not of themselves console the victims in our society. This knowledge is the pain at the heart of our best political and social efforts. We can never cease such efforts, but neither can we have any illusions about them.

Within hours of the departure of the Magi, an unknown angel came in the darkness to a sleeping Joseph and told him to leave as soon as humanly possible. It may have been a gesture of considerable personal risk, since the power of people like Herod comes from having eyes and ears everywhere. Such a warning had only to be overheard or even suspected, and a life would be forfeit. Yet someone did give the warning, and changed the future.

For someone in that village of long ago, what significance had the survival of a refugee child? To us who claim to follow the Lord born as that child, the value of that act of personal courage is incalculable. At the heart of our Christian faith is the claim that the living out of our human life by the one child snatched from Herod's death squad has brought salvation to all. One man or woman acted; one child was spared. In each case only one, but that made all the difference.

The Confession of
Saint Peter

Almighty God,
you inspired Simon Peter, first among the apostles,
to confess Jesus as Messiah and Son of the living God.
Keep your Church steadfast upon the rock of this faith,
so that in unity and peace
we may proclaim the one truth
and follow the one Lord,
who lives and reigns with you and the Holy Spirit,
one God, now and for ever.

Acts 4.8-13 or 1 Peter 5.1-4
Psalm 23
Matthew 16.13-19

ଔ

I f you decide to go to Caesarea Philippi, you are in for a
climb most of the way. If you begin the journey from
the northern end of the lake you are already on the
edge of the upper Galilee, and after a few miles the hills to
the north of the lake give way to rolling countryside. Domi-
nating the distant skyline is the white slope of Mount Hermon. If you are the driver, you are in for constant
gear-changing as you go north along the line of the Jordan as

it flows south to the lake. Toward the end of your journey you will be in high but gentle, green countryside, as far from the stark dustiness of Judea as you can get in Israel.

The Caesarea Philippi you come to today is only a memory, a tantalizing fragment of a once lively and raucous city. So little remains that you can glimpse its loveliness today only in its setting rather than in any of its substance. All that remains is the quiet whispering flow of the Jordan, forming here from the three tiny rivers that flow down from what is today the Baneas National Park. Here where you stand by the low wall overlooking the water, Roman army officers on leave took their few days or weeks of respite from an occupation that was often boring and sometimes brutal.

To look up and beyond the river is to see what was once the upper part of this city. Very little remains. If you look at certain indentations in the ridge you are seeing the remains of the many shrines to the god Pan, who was patron to this place. As is obvious from the name of the city, Pan had to share the honors with another god who was able to make more pressing claims on these people—the emperor Caesar himself.

Somewhere around here were all the activities of a garrison city—the eating places, the brothels, the theaters. It is difficult to stand here in the silence and not to hear laughter, shouting, the cries of people snatching a moment of enjoyment from lives that, because of their profession, could be short and dangerous.

We have the whole afternoon to experience this area. The time of year, the weather today, the green growth of early spring, the whisper and gurgle of the river where it forms the wide natural pool that was once the centerpiece of the city's life, all encourage us to probe back to the time when our Lord came here with a group of his disciples.

Why here, of all places, so far from their familiar haunts? I suspect it was no accident that he brought his followers here, or that he asked them that all-important question here rather than anywhere else. I suspect that Jesus decided deliberately to take them away from the security and the simplicity of the lake villages. He took them into another world, a world of Pan shrines rather than of synagogues, an urban rather than a rural world, a world of sophistication rather than of simplicity. In the midst of all this he turned and asked them the question, "Who do you say that I am?"

Because I, too, am here today, two millennia later, I realize that the same Jesus puts the same question to me in my own time. To be a late-twentieth-century Christian of my generation, born in the late 1920s, is to have the memory, real or imagined, of a simpler and less sophisticated society, of a church firmly placed in the life of society, of a society for the most part unified around common goals and hopes. In this sense I have traveled from a familiar "Capernaum" and have come at the century's end to a very different "Caesarea Philippi." Yet I must also trust that it is the same Lord Jesus who has brought me and others to this time of immense transition, just as he brought those first disciples to this place where I walk today, a place unfamiliar to them, perhaps even disturbing and threatening. I must also trust that he has brought me and my contemporaries to this late-twentieth-century world to ask us the same question he once asked that group of friends and disciples near where I am standing, "Who do you say that I am?"

I sit on a low wall near the water and take out a small Bible I have with me. I notice that our Lord asked two questions. First, "Who do people say that the Son of Man is?" They were only too ready to suggest answers, and they probably enjoyed telling Jesus what people thought of him. I can imagine Jesus listening in the detached way of someone more interested in the process of what is going on than the content. It is more than likely that he was perfectly aware of what people said about him, but he went on waiting, gauging the exact moment to cut through the babble of voices to ask the second question. I hear him ask it quietly, almost casually, with mild curiosity in his voice. "Who do you say that I am?"

It is Peter who breaks the silence. What comes from him is what they are accustomed to—a rush of spontaneous words blurted out. Yet once again, as he has done before and will do again, Peter manages to get to the heart of the matter. Somewhere around me, cutting through the sounds of a city, the raised voices, the wheels of chariots, the clatter of horses' hooves, the words of Peter were spoken and heard. "You are the Messiah, the Son of the Living God."

The buses have gone and the souvenir-sellers have left in their cars. For a short time before I also have to leave there is silence, and in this silence I must respond to the same question. I am only too aware that, like the disciples, I can answer the first question easily. If that means being articulate about the many Christologies of my world and time, the many ways men and women think of Jesus, I can do so with enjoyment and ease. But the second question is very different. Like Peter, I know that I confront a mystery I will never understand, a love that I will never deserve, a glory that I cannot comprehend. All I can do is to say quietly and privately what Peter said loudly and publicly: "You are the Messiah, the Son of the Living God."

I am well aware of the vulnerability and cost with which this faith of mine is held, but I take comfort in the fact that my brother Peter was vulnerable, too. And I am afraid of the consequences of this faith I have confessed on this low wall by a shallow pool. But then, once again, I stand beside my brother Peter. When Jesus tried to tell Peter the meaning of what he had said, of what the cost in suffering would be, Peter was unable to accept those consequences. He moved into what we would today call deep denial, so much so that his friend and Lord had to lash him back to reality.

This day is not remembered by the church merely as Saint Peter's feast day, but as what we call "the confession of Saint Peter." The church has decided to focus on a single incident in Peter's life that could not have taken more than a few short moments. But the truth is that life is punctuated by such moments, moments when we decide to choose or to speak or to act in one way rather than in another, affecting the course of our lives for months or years or even a whole lifetime ahead. For Peter the fleeting few moments in this city were such a time and such a choice. As I get ready to leave, walking toward the group that is waiting by the bus, I ask simply that my own echoing of his words may find me as faithful as my brother Peter.

The Conversion of
Saint Paul

Almighty God,
by the preaching of your servant Paul
you caused the light of the gospel
to shine throughout the world.
May we who celebrate his wonderful conversion
follow him in bearing witness to your truth;
through Jesus Christ our Lord,
who lives and reigns with you and the Holy Spirit,
one God, now and for ever.

Acts 26.9-23 or Galatians 1.11-24
Psalm 67
Matthew 10.16-22

☙

I became aware of his presence behind me as soon as I began to write—he was actually peering over my shoulder! "I wonder what they chose for my day," he said, as if talking to himself. The impression he made on me was that of a brainy man so caught up with higher things that any human company was irrelevant. Taking not the slightest notice of me, he continued to scan the texts of the three lections, all the while muttering to himself.

"Hmm—I remember that day with Agrippa. The trouble with local strongmen like him was that you never knew what was going on behind the scenes. Were you dealing with him or was the local Roman administrator pulling the strings? Or was the Jewish community breathing down his neck? Sometimes your life could depend on knowing which it was."

He reached forward to turn the page, his hand quick and nervous. No hint of apology for interrupting, no hesitation about intruding. I knew where he was when he grunted, "Those idiots! They gave me quite a time in Galatia. I should have known they would. They had a reputation for being tough and stubborn. In those mountain districts things hadn't changed for generations; they hardly knew what was happening in the rest of the world."

He flicked over to the gospel reading. "Well, thank God for that!"

"For what?" I asked, trying to keep the sharpness out of my voice. After all, he had walked into my life without making any effort at a greeting of any kind—as always, he had his plan and everyone else was expected to make it theirs.

"There." A bony finger jabbed at the page. "Those Gentiles. See where the Lord himself talks about the Gentiles. That should shut up those people who accuse me of inventing something he never intended. Of all the things said about me, that is what annoys me more than anything else, the lie that somehow I invented the church."

I decided to dispense with the social niceties, since my visitor obviously had. "Well," I said, "you must admit you had more to do than anyone else with what eventually came into being."

"So you think I invented the church?" he barked.

"No," I said in exasperation. "That is not what I'm saying. If you would only listen you would hear me paying you a compliment. The simple fact is that you played a tremendous part in forming the church as we know it today."

"Then I didn't do such a good job, did I?" Suddenly as he said this his face broke into a broad smile. He extended a hand. "Somebody told me you were trying to write something about me and I thought I would drop in. One of the things about being in the past is that people can write the most extraordinary things about you and you can't do anything about it."

My mind was racing furiously for something to start him talking again. "What's the most annoying thing ever said about you?"

He answered without a second's hesitation. "That I was always impossible to work with. Barnabas started that rumor in his own quiet, sly way. What he and the others from that part of the world could never realize was that if you were going to deal with people in the West you had to begin to think like them. You had to be organized. You couldn't meander on mentally in the way the East loves to do. You get to the point, make your ideas clear and crisp. I knew that because of the years in Tarsus. When I tried to get the others to do that, they resented it. They called me a dictator!"

He backed toward a chair and sat on the very edge of it. I guessed that was the biggest concession he ever made to comfort and I had a vision of him sitting on the edge of chairs and couches all across the Roman empire, never relaxing, never easing up.

It was time for me to be conciliatory. "You made a tremendous difference," I said, with affirmation in every syllable. "Without you the faith might never have got this far."

"Too bad nobody thought so at the time!" he responded. "The day we left Caesarea for Rome I could almost hear the Jerusalem community rubbing its palms with satisfaction that they had got rid of the troublemaker. The fact is, they were totally incapable of taking on the job."

"Why did you take it on?" I asked. I was pleased to see that he had settled back a little in the chair.

"If you want a simple answer (something you know I'm not good at)"—he smiled—"I took on the empire because I was convinced the Lord wanted me to."

He leaned forward with the Bible in his hands. "It's all there in that passage you people read on my feast day, the part about telling my story to Agrippa. Have you ever noticed how often I told that story? I told it because everything I ever became grew out of that moment and that experience. The fact that I tell it again and again is just a sign of how I despaired of ever communicating the power of that encounter. I never had a moment's doubt after that. I never doubted that everything he came for and everything he died and rose for was something bigger than a tiny province on the backside of the empire! Maybe I shouldn't put it that way, but if you had had to deal with the ignorance and narrowmindedness of some of those people...."

"You mean the people from around the lake?" I asked.

"No," he replied, "for some reason they *did* see the bigger picture. Of course Galilee always did tend to notice the bigger world. It was around Jerusalem you encountered the limited vision of those who had joined in those first early years. I think it was because Jerusalem tended to be the center of the universe for them and they had no idea it was out on the edge of things. If it weren't for James's superb leadership at the first conference, we would never have broken out of that prison of tradition. In fact, if it weren't for James I probably wouldn't have got out of the city with my life when I came back after the journeys we took. Jerusalem was my great failure. I tried my best to get money for them when times were really bad, but somehow nothing seemed to work."

The sadness in his voice made me feel helpless, and yet I wanted to offer some comfort if I could. "I'm immensely honored you thought it worth your while to come and talk to me," I said. I really meant it, but I was surprised by his response. It was given very quietly, almost as if Paul were talking to himself.

"One of the things I discovered," he said, "was that honor is easy to come by. It is much harder to be loved than to be honored. Whatever honor I earned was by being totally singlegleminded about what I was doing. The result was that I missed out on much of life—real life, that is. It was only toward the end that I realized that friends like Luke and Mark and Aquila and Priscilla stayed with me not *because* of who I was, but in *spite* of who I was. I never really figured out that love—loving and being loved—is the most important thing of all."

Trying to be comforting, I said to him, "But surely what you wrote toward the end of your first letter to the Corinthians—surely that meant you realized love was at the center of it all."

Paul smiled. "Oh yes, I knew. I knew everything—knew it here." He tapped the side of his head. "But it isn't enough to know things with your mind. You also have to know them here." He put a hand on his chest, over his heart. "When I wrote that piece to the Corinthians I was very proud of it. I never realized that someone was using my hand to write it, trying to get me to hear it myself."

His voice gathered strength. "I should go. I'm taking up your time—and getting sentimental!" He was obviously in charge again. He stood up and looked down at me in my chair. "You go back to your writing," he said with authority. I obeyed without a word. A few moments later when I looked around the room, he was gone.

The Presentation

of our Lord Jesus Christ in the Temple

Blessed are you, O Lord our God,
for you have sent us your salvation.
Inspire us by your Holy Spirit
to recognize him who is the glory of Israel
and the light for all nations,
your Son Jesus Christ our Lord.

Malachi 3.1-4

Psalm 84.1-7 or Psalm 24.7-10

Hebrews 2.14-18   *Luke 2.22-40*

ଓଃ

You can still see the steps through the high railings and locked gates that guard these fragile ruins from the countless feet of the tourists. It is possible to get permission to go in if you belong to one of the institutions of learning licensed by the government, and that is why we are standing here at the top of the great ancient staircase. There are huge gaps in the stones after the passing of centuries. At the bottom, where the ruined staircase begins, there is rubble; below that are the earthen mounds from which old stones protrude; and then we can see the busy city highway—noisy, dusty, crowded, the air heavy with gasoline and diesel. Behind us is the towering wall that today forms the southern end of the Al Aqsa mosque. Formerly it had a series of gates; today it is solid stone. The crowds came up the steps and poured through the gates onto the vast public concourse of Herod's Temple, day after day, on their way to the various temple courts.

She would certainly have come up these steps, carrying the child and with Joseph beside her. Days and weeks had gone by since she had given birth, and some strength was beginning to flow back into her body. She still tired easily, but the time had come to make the journey to present her baby to a priest. In spite of her weariness, this for her was truly a day the Lord had made and she would rejoice and be glad in it!

They reached the top of the steps and passed into the great public space. This structure was still a construction site even after forty years of building had gone by. This Temple had been started before Mary was born and it was still unfinished. Workmen here and there were putting the final touches to stone, to wood, to marble. From where she and Joseph stood facing north, the great platform of stone stretched ahead of them for nearly eight city blocks by modern reckoning. She had only to look east to the ridge of the Olives and northwest to the distant mound of Nebi Samuel to see the gleaming aqueducts bringing the tens of thousands of gallons of water needed daily for the sacrifice areas, for sanitation, for drinking, for ritual cleansing.

Mixed with her excitement was a fear of the vastness and complexity of this place. Galilee seemed far away, rural, simple, unsophisticated. Here she and Joseph knew they were peasants, far from home and dependent on her family connections in the city, vulnerable to the whims of authority, and therefore all the more dependent on each other. Everything about this huge, crowded place drew them together as they made their way toward the Temple area soaring up ahead of them. Soon they met up with other couples like themselves, other children in arms, other faces mirroring both anxiety and excitement, drawn together in a group by the common necessity of the formal presentation of a child to a priest, as Jewish law demanded.

They waited until their turn came. Back at the outer entrance Joseph had purchased the two inexpensive birds demanded by the occasion for sacrifice. There was little choice for what he could afford—either turtledoves or pigeons. He waited while she gave the child to the priest on duty in front of the altar where the red coals of the fire gleamed. The priest took the child, turned from them, and for a moment held him high above the fire. All three of them knew that they were acting out a terrible memory of the days when for a brief time their ancestors had given children to the fire in the belief that this was required by the cult of the god Moloch. The brief moment over, the priest turned, placed the child back in her arms, turned to Joseph, accepted the two birds, cut them with a single stroke of the knife, spilled the blood on the altar surface, and threw their bodies on the fire. Thus was the life of their child redeemed in blood. She was aware of his warmth and life against her body. They turned to go.

At first she was not aware of the old man half-hidden by the great pillar. He moved very slowly toward them and it seemed as if he wanted to speak to her. Putting his stick against a nearby pillar he stretched his arms toward her, obviously wanting to hold the child. Something trustworthy about the old man let her place the child in the large, gnarled hands. When he took the child, the change in him was almost instantaneous—the shuffle changed to a walk, the walk to a subdued dance. His voice rose into a kind of sing-song in which he celebrated the child's birth, a birth he had awaited for years. This child in his arms, he sang, would be "the glory of Israel and a light to the Gentiles."

Mary received the child back from him and they were both turning to go when the old man looked at her. He spoke quite clearly and with chilling emphasis. "Because of this child," he said, "a sword will pierce your heart." No sooner had he said it than he turned, picked up his stick, and moved out of sight among the pillars.

At first she wasn't sure what she heard, the statement was so unexpected and so terrifying. Mary instinctively clasped the baby as tightly as she could, and as she did so, a tiny woman, even older than the man, came toward them. Her eyes, sunken deep in the dark creases of her face, shone with friendliness and joy at the sight of the child and his mother. Introducing herself as Anna, she told them whose family she was and what tribe, then chatted on about her life here in the Temple precincts, reminiscing about her own youth, her few short years of joy as a young wife, the decision to become part of the vast Temple workforce. She took the child carefully in her arms, offered a prayer for him, then turned to show him to anyone passing by, telling them that he was certainly going to make a wonderful contribution to the world. Everything about her was joy and kindness itself. Mary wondered afterward if Anna had seen what had happened with Simeon and had deliberately set out to undo the shock and pain of his last threatening remark.

They came out at the top of the southern steps, pausing for a moment to see if they could locate the place far below where they had left the beast that had brought her and the child. As soon as they found it they began the journey south to their home in Nazareth.

I have always felt that Luke has given us an extraordinarily rich portrait of humanity in this story. There on stage, framed between the great pillars of the Temple, their faces lit by the flames of the huge altar, we have every aspect of human experience, the full spectrum of humanity that God in this child came to inhabit. At the center of everything is the child, only weeks old. He is held by his mother, herself a young adult. Beside her is Joseph, a man young in our terms, probably in his prime in that earlier time. Beside them at different moments stands age in the persons of Simeon and Anna. With Anna, who, we are told, is eighty-four, we see a rare living out of great age in that society.

All Orthodox representations of our Lord's resurrection show him hand-in-hand with Adam and Eve as he rises, lifting humanity to God. Here on this day in the Temple, the child Jesus being presented to God brings to the encounter the whole human story. The scene is also a microcosm of any community, and by contemplating it we are gently but firmly reminded that not only does every stage of life have its legitimate place before God, but there is also a sense in which the community that does not have the spectrum of life from childhood to extreme old age is somehow incomplete.

If we see the moment as I have suggested, the four adults and the child, we notice that Luke is drawing a subtle parallel. If the two younger people embody physical life and physical creativity, the two older embody quite another kind of creativity, that of the mind and the spirit. Mary and Joseph see the child with the adoring eyes of those to whom the child has been given; Simeon and Anna see him as icon—they see what the child means. The younger eyes look at the child, the older eyes look through him. This gift of looking through rather than merely at is one of God's greatest gifts to us. It is the priceless gift that, all unknowingly, both Simeon and Anna brought to this moment in the Temple.

Saint Joseph
of Nazareth

O God,
from the family of your servant David
you raised up Joseph
to be the guardian of your incarnate Son.
Give us grace to follow him
in faithful obedience to your commands;
through Jesus Christ our Lord,
who lives and reigns with you and the Holy Spirit,
one God, now and for ever.

2 Samuel 7.4, 8-16 or Romans 4.13-18
Psalm 89.1-4, 26-29
Luke 2.41-52

❧

I looked across the cafeteria tables and saw him. He was on his own and he was having difficulty balancing his tray because he was also carrying a heavy metal box; like me, he must have been grabbing lunch in between appointments. Something about him intrigued me so much that I decided to ask him if he minded sharing the small table. As I headed toward him, I suddenly knew without any doubt that his name would be Joseph and that the metal box he had with him contained carpenter's tools.

I was right, although I could hardly believe it at the time. It became even more mysterious when I found that in some way he was expecting me, or at least expecting someone.

The first thing he wanted to do was set the record straight about his age. "I don't know of a single portrait of me in any art gallery in the world where I am not completely senile!" he complained, laughing. "Believe me, I've looked in every one of them. There I am every time, heavy beard, bent over, shuffling around, trying to keep up. How do you think I supported my family? Every day I wrestled with big pieces of wood, sawed them, lifted them, hung doors, and so on. How do they think I weathered a long hard journey down the coast road across the northern Sinai when we had to get out quickly and run for safety only days after the baby was born?"

He looked at me hard. "Do you remember when we lost him on that visit to Jerusalem? We were three days out from the city. Know what that means? It means we had gone down over the escarpment on the Roman road, down by the Wadi Kelt into the Jericho plain, and were just about to turn north for home. Have you any idea what it means to climb back up there a second time, your heart in your mouth? You do that only if you're young and hardy and healthy. If I had been the old man I'm supposed to have been I wouldn't have been able to drag myself up the Temple steps, let alone chase around half the city!"

I asked him about the early days, the time it all began. "Actually Matthew got it right," he said. "You remember he begins his book by describing how I felt when she told me she was pregnant. I was devastated. Put yourself in my place. In the world you live in these things can be understood much more easily, but it was very different for us. The consequences could have been horrendous, especially for her. I was so appalled I couldn't speak to her for days. I couldn't work—I even closed up the shop. I didn't want to meet anyone. I went off and swore at God. Anyone who heard me—and I took care nobody did in those hills—would have thought I was going crazy. In a sense it was because I loved her so much, and in the end that made the difference. I just decided that if she said things were this way, then that's the way they must be. End of story. I went back. I told her I would stay with her and you know the rest."

I pushed him a bit. "Was it really that simple?" I asked.

"Well, yes and no," he replied. "I guess it was a dream I had the second or third night out. Something or someone came to me and said that everything was going to be all right, that her child was going to be—well, different, special somehow. I don't exactly know how to say it. In this dream I was being told to name the child, and somehow I knew that meant accepting the child. It wasn't enough for him to arrive into Mary's arms. I had to stretch mine out for him, too."

He leaned back in his chair and stretched his arms on the table, his great, dark, strong hands facing up. I looked at them, knowing how securely and yet gently they could hold a newborn. We were silent for a few moments. I knew he was remembering. Into the silence I said very softly, "What was she like?"

He looked at me as if he was looking for a way to reply. Then, defeated by the task, he said simply, "I loved her the first time I ever saw her and I loved her till the day I died."

"Why do you disappear from the story right after you came back from that visit to Jerusalem? He was just twelve then, wasn't he?"

"Simple," he said. "I had an accident. I used to get contracts in various places. At the time all of us in the Galilee had been given a real break by Herod's building program over in Sepphoris. The work site was only about an hour away and the money was good—until I fell off some scaffolding. I knew it was all over even as they were carrying me back. I could hardly feel a thing and I knew enough to know what *that* meant. I died in just a few days. The real agony for me was knowing how awful it was going to be for her and the children. And yet, I can remember how it made all the difference, having him. Even though he was only fifteen or so I knew that he would be able to take over. He and she together would get the rest of the kids through. That at least made it bearable."

"Tell me," I said hesitantly, "did you ever wonder how things were going to go later in his life?" He looked at me, again searching for a way to reply. "I always knew things would never be ordinary for him. We used to talk a lot, you know, especially after that trip south to Jerusalem when he was twelve. Things weren't the same between us after that. Mary and I both saw something in him that day that—what shall I say?—made us afraid. It's hard to say what it was."

He paused and looked around him, then said, "There was something that day in his voice, in his eyes, I will never forget. I remember feeling that our son was no longer ours, that he was someone else's. In fact, I think it was at that moment I knew for the first time what Mary had meant when she had told me the news of his being inside her, when she said that the child wasn't mine."

I said nothing because I had nothing to say.

"I read what they wrote about him later on. Do you know the one thing that has made it all worthwhile for me? What he succeeded in communicating more clearly than almost anything else was the closeness he felt to God. People could see that in everything he did and said. I can only begin to understand how offended some of those rabbis were when they heard him call God *Abba.*" He paused to gather his feelings together.

"Did he call you that sometimes?" I asked quietly.

"Yes," he said, "he would say that when he was a kid. He knew I liked it."

"So his sense of intimacy with God is something he must have learned from being close to you," I suggested.

Joseph's whole demeanor changed. His eyes cleared, the smile was back. "That's what I was going to talk about. It makes everything worthwhile for me, knowing that I gave him that, showed him what a father could be. I may not have been able to give him much of this world's goods but at least I gave him that."

"You did," I said, deeply moved. "You gave him that and you've given it to millions of people ever since, including me. The two of you gave us a portrait of God that invites utter intimacy with his children."

Suddenly embarrassed by my speech, I groped for our two cups and asked if he would like a refill. Not waiting for an answer, I threaded my way to the counter and got the coffee. When I got back to the table he had gone. I thought of running after him but then thought better of it. I knew that he had done what he came to do. He had told the story his way.

The Annunciation

of Our Lord Jesus Christ to the Blessed Virgin Mary

Pour your grace into our hearts, O Lord,
that we who have known the incarnation
of your Son Jesus Christ,
announced by an angel to the Virgin Mary,
may by his cross and passion
be brought to the glory of his resurrection;
who lives and reigns with you,
in the unity of the Holy Spirit,
one God, now and for ever.

Isaiah 7.10-14

Psalm 40.5-10 or Psalm 45

Hebrews 10.4-10   Luke 1.26-38

ॐ

T he old well is nowhere in sight, yet you know this is the place. Archeology has firmly established that the place where you are standing is the northern end of that tiny village street that was once first-century Nazareth. The well of that quiet village, now a huge bustling city, has had long use over the centuries. Built at the intersection of two main streets, the well now has a few seats set into its wall. An iron fixture sticks out of the ground and pieces of paper litter the sidewalk, but this is the well she once knew and from which she would have drawn their water.

What strikes you as you approach the well is the thought that if the angel Gabriel decided to contact anyone here these days, he would have to shout at the top of his lungs! But perhaps it wasn't that much different in her day. We like to think of the meeting between Mary and the angel as taking place in serene surroundings, but there would have been the children at play, the sheep and the goats with their eternal bleating, the camels with their deep, coughing grunts, the merchants shouting out their wares. Today the traffic is approaching gridlock and the air is reeking with fumes. This is late-twentieth-century Nazareth, very alive, crowded, busy, and prosperous, the Arab city in the valley and on the western hills, the Jewish city on the eastern hillsides.

For some reason, perhaps a story told me as a child, in my imagination I place Mary in this spot for her encounter with the angel. In her day this bowl in the hills would have been empty except for her village lying at its heart. The hillsides would have been open, green, and still. I try to see the street as she would have seen it, the small houses not so different from some of the tiny homes in the back streets of Nazareth today: the rough wooden door, the opening for light and air, the flat roof, the animals outside, a farm implement leaning against a wall. To her it would have been her ordinary, everyday world. She did not expect a visit from beyond that ordinary world. Like her, I have no such expectations. If it were to happen to me, I would know only one reaction—like her, I would be afraid.

I find myself wondering where Luke found her when he came to her long ago and asked for her memories to record

in his book. Not here. For one thing, her days of drawing
water from the well would have been long over by the time
he met her: that task would have passed to her daughters-in-
law. But there may have been another reason. From the day
her son became a public figure there was less and less to
keep her in Nazareth. In fact, there may have been good reason to leave. He had returned to the town once and spoken
in the synagogue. Her pride had turned to horror when she
felt the waves of anger toward him. The incident had nearly
resulted in his being killed, and what had hurt her most was
seeing so many of her neighbors in the hostile crowd. That
may have been the point at which she decided to leave, or
perhaps the decision was made for her by the family. So by
the time Luke met her she was probably in Jerusalem, sitting in the few square feet of shadow and light that would
have been hers as a lodger in the house of John the beloved
disciple.

I think of how Luke's angelic messenger reassured her,
telling her not to be afraid. The fear must have appeared in
her eyes; her whole being must have said no at first. Her
first word to the messenger must have been a desperate effort to break the spell, to reassure herself that this was a
dream at midday. We can never know in what tone and with
what inflection she said the words, "How can this be, since I
am a virgin?" Lightly, with laughing disbelief? Acidly, with
the earthy vehemence of a rural woman? However she said
it, she wields the statement as a weapon against this assault
on her credulity, her sense of the normal, her very life itself.
Not until she sees its total lack of effect on the messenger
does she allow herself to enter into this waking dream that
ceases to be a dream and takes on a reality that will last forever.

There are echoes of her face in those of the young women
on the nearby busy crosswalk, or shopping in the stores, or

waiting in their cars for a light to change. It reminds me of how important it is to keep the long association with sacred places, to keep open the long roads winding back through time. Even here in this most unpromising of settings, this Nazareth of today so taken up with its complex and even dangerous present, she reaches out and touches me.

She comes gently to me, a clear inner voice apart from all the surrounding noise. "Why have you come to Nazareth?" she inquires.

The question is so direct and simple I don't know what to say at first. My answers seem miserably inadequate. To take part in a college program? To lecture other clergy? To gather material for a book? "All of these reasons are true," I tell her. "I can't help them. They are what my life is about."

Standing right in front of me, she only smiles as I continue. "And I am here—we're all here—because of your son. We know him but we don't know him. We have found him but we continually lose him. We are here searching for him."

"It's good that you come," she replies, "as long as you realize you don't have to come here. He isn't just here, you know. He is where you are. You know this, don't you?" She asks it very gently, as if I were a child.

"Yes," I reply. "I know that. Down deep I know it, but I still have to search for him."

She changes the subject. "Giving birth to him taught me something about God. I learned it from the first moment I held my son in my arms. I learned that God comes in the most ordinary ways and in the most ordinary things and at the most ordinary moments. I tell you this because people think they know it but they don't, really. They want a mysterious and majestic God. The strange thing is that God is like that, but the mystery and the majesty are always disguised by the ordinary, and most people can't see through the disguise."

25 March

Just as I can't be sure when she came, I can't be sure when she went from me. Even to say that she came and went doesn't begin to describe the experience of being encountered by her. There was no outward change, no lessening of traffic, no silencing of the noise. It would be true to say that she made use of all the surrounding reality to come to me, just as her son Jesus does each day of my life. And while it is true to say that her presence left me, it is also true that I could no more leave her in Nazareth than I could leave her son, who is my Lord.

Saint Mark

Almighty God,
by the hand of Mark the evangelist
you gave to your Church
the gospel of Jesus Christ, the Son of God.
We thank you for his witness,
and pray that we may be grounded firmly in its truth;
through Jesus Christ our Lord,
who is alive and reigns with you and the Holy Spirit,
one God, now and for ever.

Isaiah 52.7-10 or Ephesians 4.7-8, 11-16
Psalm 2.7-13
Mark 1.1-15 or Mark 16.15-20

ൠ

From time to time people will ask me how I manage to run into people from the New Testament. I realize that by putting it that way I make the New Testament sound like a foreign country or territory, and in some ways I suppose it is, at least for a Christian. It is a land we have available to us to visit from time to time where we know a great many people. We don't know them intimately, but we do know something about them, and even if we don't realize it we have formed images of them in our minds. We have made them into people, at least on our terms.

Since I expect to meet them, I often do. Wherever I go, I look out for them. I will look at a certain person next to me, wherever I happen to be, and ask myself, "Could that be Luke? Could that be Mary Magdalene, Barnabas, Paul?" I carry mental portraits of such people around with me, and although you may not realize it, so do you. All Christians do, to one degree or another.

I saw Saint Mark one day as I sat in a lecture being given by a very earnest and rather dull professor. The subject was a perennial one: "Who is Jesus Christ today?" Halfway through I became aware of a young student sitting not far away from me who was becoming more and more restless, shaking his head and shifting in his seat as the lecturer droned on. His whole demeanor seemed to be crying out "No!" Afterward, when I went over to talk to him, that is exactly the word he burst out with when I asked him his opinion of the lecture.

"No!" he exploded. "It wasn't like that at all. He wasn't like that and neither was Peter or any of the rest of them. That isn't how it happened and I never said any of that when I wrote about it!"

I could not help thinking how easily Mark fitted into this campus setting. He was still in his twenties, brimming over with energy, expressing all his opinions and convictions with passion. It was obvious why the book he wrote is pulsating with energetic verbs, rushing from one quick scene to the next, sweeping the reader through its pages.

"Tell me," I said, as if this were the most natural of conversations, "what it was that triggered your writing the book in the first place."

Without a moment's hesitation he answered, "Peter. He always wanted me to do it. He wouldn't let me alone until I did, and he gave me endless material, far more than I could use." (I yearned to ask Mark what happened to the stories he didn't use, but somehow I knew I shouldn't.)

"It was Peter who pointed out to me," Mark went on, "that none of us was getting any younger and time was slipping by. He was wise enough to realize that memory tends to play funny tricks with events, so he felt it was important that somebody should write something."

He paused. "There was another reason, too. Other people were beginning to write things down. Someone whose name I've forgotten put together a long list of the Master's sayings—just a collection of things Jesus had said from time to time. You people today might call it a collection of sound bytes." I tried not to look startled at the vivid slang. "That material was very useful to me when I began to figure out the shape of my book."

"I don't blame Peter for pushing you," I said. "After all, you were an ideal person to do the job. Very few people had your credentials: you grew up in the Jerusalem area, you spent time with Paul, your house was a gathering place for the community. Do you remember much about those very early days in the Jerusalem area?"

"Yes and no," he said. "I was just a kid, but I remember a visitor who used to come to our house from time to time. He wasn't in the city very often, but the memory of those visits stands out in my mind. I remember the night they all came with him and used part of the house for Passover. I remember it because my mother was crying and she wouldn't tell me why, though by that time I was old enough to know that something wasn't right. I could see it in all the faces of Jesus' friends as I let them in. About halfway through the evening one of them left the room upstairs where they had gathered, raced through the house, and disappeared without saying a word."

"Your house became key to the whole thing, didn't it?" I prompted.

"They needed a place like ours because so many of them were from out of town. After a while the guys I went around with kept giving me a hard time, telling me I had a Galilean accent." He laughed. "Mother didn't like that one bit. Like most people brought up in Jerusalem, she thought anyone from the Galilee was a hick."

His voice changed. "Of course, she didn't think that about the Master. From the beginning there was something different about him. You could tell he was from the north, but when you were with him, where he came from didn't seem to matter. There was something about him—it's hard to say what it was—that gave you the feeling he was in charge. That's what you noticed about him."

Because I had often read his book, I knew the man on the other side of the table was full of energy and restless. I was afraid he might suddenly say, "Time to go," and head out. "What about Paul—working with him, I mean. What was it like?"

Without a moment's hesitation, he grinned and said, "Terrible. He was an impossible person. The most demanding so-and-so I ever met."

"Was he really mad at you when you became homesick in Perga in Pamphylia and wanted to go back?" I asked.

Mark grinned again at the memory. "He was livid. After all, I had been allowed to come with him and my uncle Barnabas against Paul's better judgment, and, being Paul, he said so in no uncertain terms. I suspect he had paid at least part of my expenses himself, and in those days a group of three men was a little more secure than two when you headed in from the coast of—what do you call it these days?"

"Turkey," I said.

"So there we were, five hundred miles from home, and me saying enough's enough! No wonder Paul was mad. Let's face it, I deserved it."

His voice and his expression changed, and he looked a little sad. "What I don't think I deserved was to be cut out of things for the next twenty years. Actually, I was never entirely out of things; I never stopped picking up information and gathering stories. I was good at that. But as far as Paul was concerned I had let him down, and there was no room in Paul's life for people who did that."

"But you hung in," I said. "Why?"

"Well, I guess there were several reasons. First, I'm naturally stubborn. I was determined to prove to Paul that he had been wrong about me. From time to time when we would meet I would make it my business to show him I was still around, still involved. Little by little I wore him down. You know his letter to the folk in Thessalonica?" I nodded. "And the short personal letter he wrote to Philemon?" Again I nodded. Mark was obviously pleased. "Then you've noticed how he mentions me specially. I remember when someone showed me those letters for the first time and I knew I was back in his good graces. That was a big day for me."

I asked him if he wanted to go over to the cafeteria for a cup of coffee, but he said no, that he had to go. I was desperate to hang on to him. "You said there were several reasons you stayed involved. What were the others?"

In a quieter voice he said, "Peter. He made the difference. Not that we met very often. He traveled a great deal and so did I—all of us who had been at the center of things had to travel in those days. Every new local community wanted one of us to spend some time with them. But when Peter and I did meet there seemed to be a bond between us in spite of the age difference. We would spend hours together. For the most part he would speak and I would listen. With Peter I went through the few years they had had together—in my imagination, I mean. The stories, the incidents, the crises, the healings, the confrontations. He told me everything. Sometimes when he would speak of the last few days he would break off now and then, but he would take it up again, almost as if he knew this was the only way to make sure the story got passed on."

Again Mark paused. I could feel he was going away from me in some way I couldn't understand, but I knew I would have to let him go.

"You said there was something else. What was it?" Mark grew even quieter, as if what he was trying to say meant so much to him that there was only one way he could say it.

"You really want to know why I hung in?" he asked. "For the same reason you and countless others have. I hung in for the same reason that it is possible for me to meet you here two thousand years after I wrote my gospel. It's because of him, the Master. Isn't it the same for you?"

He looked at me. "Yes," I said quietly.

I knew it was time, and we both stood up. He looked at me and said a single word: "Peace." I echoed it. He turned and I watched him climb quickly up the stairs to the door of the lecture hall. With a strong pull of the handle he opened the door, and suddenly he was gone.

Saint Philip &
Saint James

Almighty God,
you gave to your apostles Philip and James
grace and strength to bear witness to the truth.
Grant that we, mindful of their victory of faith,
may glorify in life and death the name of Jesus Christ,
who lives and reigns with you and the Holy Spirit,
one God, now and for ever.

Isaiah 30.18-21 or 2 Corinthians 4.1-6
Psalm 119.33-40
John 14.6-14

☙

"Nowadays," I said to Philip, "we always remember you on the same day we remember another of the group—James. Why is that? How did it happen that you two got linked in Christian memory?" At first he looked a bit mystified, but then he brightened and said, "Do you think people have come to think of me as a real insider, up there with Peter and James and John?" I hated to dampen the hopeful note in his voice.

"Well, actually," I had to say, "it's not *that* James you're linked with."

Philip's face fell a little. "You mean the James who was Alphaeus's son? Why do you commemorate *him*, anyway?"

"I don't know," I had to admit. "We don't know a thing about him except that he was going around with the rest of you." I could tell he was not too pleased by this link with James and decided not to make things worse by adding that his companion on the calendar of saints had since become known as James the Less.

I met Philip as we both came out of a Sunday morning eucharist in a large suburban church. I was on business in the city and knew the rector, so I had taken a taxi out to the suburbs. Philip seemed like a gentle sort of person—pleasant, but otherwise unremarkable. He saw that I was a visitor when I arrived, gave me a warm handshake, and later suggested I might like to sit with him. After the service he had suggested we go to the coffee hour. Wary, I made a snide remark about church coffee hours, and just at that moment, a funny thing happened. He turned, looked right at me, and said, "Come and see." Not only did we go to coffee hour, but after that we went to have a sandwich together.

"When you told me, 'Come and see,' were you giving me a kind of signal?" I asked.

"Yes," he said, smiling. "I knew you would get it. I knew you would remember I said that to Nathanael the day he tried to brush me off with his crass remark about nothing good coming out of Nazareth."

"I've often wondered why you didn't tell him where to go that day. You must have felt like it," I said. Philip shook his head. "No. It wasn't important. That was a joke that was going around at that time. He was from Cana, and Jesus, as you know, came from Nazareth. Those two towns were intense rivals; today they would probably have had rival football teams. I knew he didn't mean anything nasty. I also knew him well enough to know that he would come if I invited him. He did, and he never regretted it."

He paused as if wondering whether to keep going, and then he added, "You know, as we watch you people these days trying to get more people interested in the Master, we are always amazed at the way you hang back from inviting others in, even your friends."

I hastily changed the subject. "These days—and not only these days but for centuries—when we commemorate saints like you, we select pieces of scripture. One of the pieces picked for you, from Isaiah's prophecy, was in today's bulletin."

Philip nodded. "I know why they picked that for me," he said. "At least I think I do. See these words, 'Your eyes shall see your Teacher'? Israel has been through a long exile and everyone is wondering what its meaning can possibly be. Does God care? Does life and human experience really mean anything? That's what is being wrestled with in this passage. In all this doubt and groping Isaiah assures them that somehow the face of God will swim into focus. That's how I heard the passage this morning, probably because this is what happened to me. From the very first moment I met the Master, somehow I knew who he was."

I knew from his voice that he was launched on his story. All I had to say was, "Tell me how you met him," and Philip was off running.

"It was down south," he began, "down where the Jordan ends up in the Dead Sea. I was there because John the baptizer was there. A few of us had been going around with him for a while, looking for something, but we were beginning to feel that John, fiery though he was, wasn't the answer. He knew that as well as we did, and he was too honest to deny it. One day he actually pointed to Jesus, who was in the same area at the time, and said a strange thing. 'See him? You're looking at the Lamb of God.' Not another word. We were not even sure what he meant, but we instinctively set out after Jesus.

"We didn't know how to make an approach, so he did it for us. He turned and in a very easy and relaxed way asked us a question I will never forget. He said, 'What are you looking for?'"

Philip looked at me. "Have you ever been asked that?" I shook my head. "Suddenly neither of us knew what to say. We stood there like idiots. I blurted out something stupid like, 'Where are you staying?' He smiled and just said, 'Come and see.' All the time he was easy, cool, relaxed, almost a little amused at us."

"And the next day you said the same thing to Nathanael, 'Come and see.'"

"I never forgot the power of that simple invitation. I often used it afterward. I remember a couple of years later a group of Greeks came looking for Jesus. I probably used the same phrase to them before taking them to Andrew, who always arranged those things."

"I have always been grateful to you," I told him, "for the moment on that last night when Jesus was talking about the Father and everyone was mystified, and you broke in with what everyone wanted to say. You said, 'Show us the Father.'"

"Yes," Philip said, "and I wished I'd kept quiet. It wasn't a good time to interrupt, but it came out before I could stop it. The Master looked terrible that night. He was completely exhausted and, I realize now, he was terrified. He looked at me and said very quietly—I remember he even used my name, which moved me deeply—'Philip, whoever has seen me has seen the Father.' Of course it didn't sink in then. It took years for that to sink in."

His voice and his eyes dropped, and I knew he was back in another room at another table. Then he looked up at me and said, "I'm glad that stayed in the record. I'm glad it means so much to you people now." There was silence. We both played with our coffee mugs.

Philip still could not leave that memory. "You have no idea how bad I felt," he said softly, "especially when he told me I just didn't know him, even after being with him for so long."

I wanted to comfort him. "But what he said to you is the heart of the whole thing. It's the heart of what we have believed about him ever since."

"I know that now. Do you remember when Jesus said to me, 'The one who believes in me will also do the works that I do'? I thought about that for a long time afterward. You see, I was nothing special in the first place, with very little to offer. To this day I cannot imagine why he was interested in me and why he made me one of the circle. But the Master meant so much to me that almost in spite of myself I managed to be useful in the following years, and I played my part in the communities that began to spread. I guess I had a way of welcoming people, making them feel wanted, introducing them to others. I think that was what I contributed more than anything else. We can't all be heroic, can we?"

"No, we can't," I said, "and thank God we don't have to be." We both looked across the table at each other and laughed. We finished our coffee, and as we went out together into the street, just to make conversation I asked him, "Do you live around here?" He shrugged, smiled, and started off down the street. "When you have time," he called back over his shoulder, "come and see."

Saint John

the Evangelist

Shed upon your Church, O Lord,
the brightness of your light,
that we being illumined by the teaching
of your apostle and evangelist John,
may walk in the light of your truth,
and come at last to the fullness of eternal life;
through Jesus Christ our Lord,
who lives and reigns with you and the Holy Spirit,
one God, now and for ever.

Genesis 1.1-5, 12-19 or 1 John 1.1-9
Psalm 92.1-2, 11-14
John 20.1-8

ೞ

M ore than any other of the gospel writers, John gives us a sense of "being there." If the actual writer is not John the son of Zebedee, who knew Jesus and traveled with him, but is simply someone passing on to us the thoughts of that most intimate of disciples, then he is a consummate reporter. There are certain things no other gospel writer does as well.

No other gospel takes us so convincingly to the Temple area and allows us to overhear the brutal confrontations between Jesus and the crowds. Only through John do we begin to understand how desperately important it was for Jesus to have access to the house in Bethany at the end of each of these terrible days. As often as I walk or drive around the south side of the Mount of Olives toward the suburb of Bethany—El Azariah as it is called in Arabic—I sense the longing with which he must have walked this same road, bathed in the warm spring sunset flooding across the western hills behind him.

Even today, two millennia after the harsh and challenging voices rang in his ears in the Temple area, it is possible to capture the echo of those confrontations. Standing here by the entrance to the Al Aqsa mosque, looking north to the exquisite beauty of the Dome of the Rock, you are aware of the potential instability of this place. Every day here the pilgrim flood goes by and the police carefully check every possible hiding place for a concealed weapon. Every day the army patrols guard the entrances; on the great stone space itself official Islamic overseers watch for any infringement of decorum and modesty. Almost every day there are minor confrontations, resentments expressed, curt directions shouted, the hurts of minor misunderstandings. In spite of all these precautions this area has on more than one occasion exploded into screaming and bloody encounter. Anyone who has spent any time here can never again read John's description of our Lord's struggle with hostile crowds without feeling the edge of fear, the ever-present possibility of things slipping out of control.

We owe John more than we can ever calculate for two decisions he made, two insights that dictated the way he wrote his gospel and the material he used. Before he even put pen to paper, three invaluable portraits of the Lord were already circulating among the communities, those of Mark, Matthew, and Luke. By the time John came to his task the whole Christian movement was poised at a threshold where it could either crash or soar. Chiefly due to the work of Paul, it was breaking out of the limitations of the small world of the eastern Mediterranean where it had been born, even though Paul was now long dead.

John saw that merely to remember the events, important as they were, would not be enough. Memory fades with time. John saw that the Jesus of the lakeside, the Jesus who was a figure in time and history, was much more than a memory. So, like an infinitely gifted surgeon placing a healthy beating heart into a body beginning to flag, he took the Jesus of the little world of the lakeshore and placed him in the human heart and mind as the eternal Christ.

John's second great insight was his choice of language. Knowing that he was aiming his work at the Greco-Roman world of his time, he used words that he knew would resonate deeply in the mind of that whole culture. He called Jesus the Son of God, knowing that this term was frequently used of those whose lives were thought to be of extraordinary significance and power.

If John the son of Zebedee himself wrote this book, then his gift to us is his presence through most of the events he records. No other account takes us so deeply into the last hours shared by Jesus and the disciples. As we read the chapters dealing with these hours, hearing Jesus unburdening himself to his friends in long soliloquies, we cannot help asking why John has remembered so much that the others have left out. Perhaps it is because none of the others—Mark, Luke, or the person who wrote the gospel we call Matthew—were there. So far as we know this is true. Mark received most of his material from the aging Peter, and both Matthew and Luke include most of it in their books. I can-

not help but think that this gives us a clue. The doorway to
all three gospels is Peter's memory. Is there some reason why
Peter does not remember those hours as John does?

Think of those hours as Peter might have experienced
them. On at least three occasions he either speaks or acts in
a way he must have deeply regretted. At a certain stage in
the evening Jesus goes to the doorway, takes the pail of
water and the cloth, kneels in front of Peter and reaches for
his foot. Peter totally misunderstands. He is so appalled,
embarrassed, and angry that Jesus has to demand his obedience. Later in the evening Jesus speaks of a coming betrayal.
Peter indignantly blusters a denial of the very possibility of
his doing such a thing. Twice in the evening this happens,
each time drawing a sharp reply from Jesus.

It is hard not to suspect that Peter dealt with the pain of
those moments in a way familiar to us all: he repressed the
memories of much about those hours. When the mature Peter came to sit down with the young Mark, his memories
flowed, but only from a certain level. John, not having had
any comparable painful experiences in those hours, remembered more deeply and completely, and we are the richer for
it.

We are given a revealing glimpse of the relationship of
Peter and John toward the end of John's gospel. We are back
on the lakeshore in the dawn. The fire blazes, breakfast
cooks on the grill. The risen Lord has called Peter aside.
Slowly and gently, like a surgeon treating a deep wound and
then sewing up the aching limb, Jesus gives Peter back his
vocation as leader of the group. He is to tend the Lord's
sheep. This conversation is about to end when John moves
across the shoreline toward them. Immediately Peter is wary.
Here is someone younger than he, bringing very different
gifts. There is a strong hint of mistrust, even fear. The risen
Lord has to reassure Peter again that he is valued and

needed. He and John are neither superior nor inferior to each other. They are different. They are both valuable instruments for the work that must be done. For this fleeting moment a veil is lifted and we are allowed to see something very poignant within their relationship.

Even in his ending John is infinitely graceful. More than any of the others he is aware that he is trying to give expression to an elusive and almost inexpressible mystery. I wonder sometimes if he was tempted to end as he began, with a passage of lyrical prose on the edge of sheer poetry. In his admission of defeat at trying to do justice to the mystery of his Lord and ours, there is a haunting quality. "There are also many other things that Jesus did; if every one of them were written down, I suppose that the world itself could not contain the books that would be written." And thus he ended his book.

Saint Matthias

Almighty God,
who in the place of Judas
chose Matthias to be numbered in the twelve,
preserve your Church from false apostles,
and by the ministry of faithful pastors and teachers
keep us steadfast in your truth;
through Jesus Christ our Lord,
who lives and reigns with you and the Holy Spirit,
one God, now and for ever.

Acts 1.15-26 or Philippians 3.13b-22
Psalm 15
John 15.1, 6-16

❧

All we know is that his name was Matthias and that for some reason he was chosen to replace the traitor Judas in the circle of Jesus' apostles. It is interesting that the writer of the collect for this day seems to worry that we will not know who is being referred to, so he links his name to that of Judas. Poor Matthias! The only way he manages to hang on in the cast of the early church drama is by being linked to the villain of the play. He is rather like the actor who has to play two parts because the first role has ended before the second begins.

Even before his election, Matthias has in some sense been put in his place. On this occasion, Luke is reporting Peter's short speech before a gathering one hundred and twenty strong. Peter refers first to the tragic fate of Judas, then says that the single criteria for this election of a successor is that the candidate be "one of the men who have accompanied us during all the time that the Lord went in and out among us, beginning from the baptism of John until the day when he was taken up from us." It brings home the fact that all four gospels are like movies with all sorts of "extras" moving in the background right from the beginning; only the disciples are constantly before the camera. Other particular "small parts"—a person who is healed or who asks a question from the crowd—swim into focus for a moment and then return to the vague background. But even farther from the camera are the group we now see being looked over by Peter and the others of what has become "the eleven." They have all been part of the drama since that distant day by the river with John the Baptist, yet not one of them has ever come into focus for us. Now for a fleeting moment a single verse in Luke's script opens a door and gives us a glimpse of them. Only two are named, Matthias and Justus, or, as he was sometimes called, Barsabbas.

Who else was there? Surely they did not simply disappear from the life of the community after this election. Many people form the cast of the Acts of the Apostles in the busy, turbulent years ahead of this community. Many more turn up in the letters of Paul. Were any of them there at this moment? We will never know, but it is intriguing to wonder.

And what of Matthias and Justus as they wait for the result of the vote? Given that culture, the election must have included a long and loud free-for-all with waving hands and fierce arguments in favor of this one or that one. Who finally brings it all to order and asks for two to be nominated? Probably Peter. For some reason I see him bringing the two candidates out of the crowd, presenting them, if only for the fact that they are anything but well known. The lots are cast, the verdict is announced. Matthias is in, Justus is out. A ragged round of applause, some mutterings of dissent, and the meeting goes on. Matthias and Justus move back into the crowd, their fifteen minutes of fame behind them forever. Never again does either man come into focus for us. Not a single action is reported, not a single word.

I have a feeling that Matthias turns up many times in our lives. He is the person who just failed to get into the photograph; either he was not there when it was taken or he stood behind someone taller or bigger. Matthias is the new neighbor we have glimpsed only once; is he worth getting to know? Or is he the person we have met only briefly, and yet when he walks out of our lives forever we are intrigued and haunted?

Matthias turns up many times in the lives of parish churches, especially in the very large ones, the kind we call corporate parishes these days. These are the people that you never really get to know beyond the shake of the hand at coffee hour, the exchange of smiles. At first she may volunteer her name, but somehow it never settles in your mind and she remains anonymous in her quiet, faithful way. Months, even years, go by until something happens or something is said that makes you realize that there is within this person a very great soul. Perhaps it turns out that the whole congregation comes to realize that hidden within its life is someone whose courage or faithfulness or generosity puts others to shame. I call someone like that my Matthias.

I have a modest hunch about Matthias that I want to share. I have a feeling that the one thing the apostles were

not looking for that day when they cast their lots was someone extraordinary. The reason is simple: I think that the one
thing that had dawned on Jesus' disciples by the time Matthias was elected was that Jesus had not called them to himself because of any extraordinary qualities—some of them
found this out the hard way—but precisely because they
were rather ordinary human beings in whom he had seen
something.

I suspect that Matthias had done only one thing: he had
shown that he could hang in there when things got tough.
This may well be the reason why the word "faithful" is used
twice about Matthias in the few short lines of his collect,
and it is even clearer when we look at the scriptures that the
church has linked with Matthias's day. Let's listen again to
Peter as he refers to "the men who have accompanied us
during all the time that the Lord Jesus went in and out
among us." Right away that tells us that Matthias was prepared to remain with a community even though he did not
get special treatment. He was simply one of the crowd.
Were it not for such men and women the church would
come apart at the seams! Indeed, such people *are* the seams
of the church.

Let's look over Paul's shoulder as he writes to the community in Philippi to tell them that becoming a Christian is
not a prize given to those who arrive at some exalted spiritual height. Rather, it is about "straining forward to what
lies ahead," and what lies ahead is "the prize of the heavenly
call of God in Christ Jesus." Our Lord, says Paul, "will trans-
form the body of our humiliation." Through this scripture
the church is trying to say to us that Matthias was elected
not for what he had been, but for what he was capable of
becoming. In giving us this intuition about Matthias, the
church is also trying to tell the rest of us something very important and very encouraging. To be told that Matthias was

elected for his possibilities is about the best news any of us could hear, because the truth is that very few of us are all that proud of what we have been to this point! To be told that God is prepared to remain faithful to us for what we may yet become opens our whole future to new possibility.

A last glance into another of today's scriptures. John's gospel lets us into the upper room, and as we stand there in the shadows we hear one word coming from Jesus again and again. What does Jesus say? Within less than a minute he uses the word "abide" no less than seven times. With only a few hours to go before his death he is expressing the heart of what discipleship is about. It is not about short-lived enthusiasms or skipping from one community to another for a change of scene, or about making promises we are not prepared to keep. Discipleship is about abiding.

It is not a word we use a great deal these days, and hearing it again reminds me of a moment in my ministry I have never forgotten. I am standing in front of the choir before my first Sunday service in my first large parish. We say the prayer and turn to move toward the sanctuary. As the last of the choir passes me, a slightly built man who seemed old to me back then says to me very softly, "Gerda and I are both in the choir. We'll stick by you no matter what." In the language of scripture, he is telling me that they will "abide" with me through thick and thin.

I do not know where or how they are now that many years have passed, but I do know that in them I encountered the spirit of Matthias—generous, quiet faithfulness.

The Visit

of the Blessed Virgin Mary
to Elizabeth

Almighty God,
who looked with favour on your servant Mary,
and called her to be the mother of your Son,
nurture in us the humility and gentleness
that found favour in your sight,
that with her we may proclaim the greatness of your name
and find the mercy you show to those who fear you;
through Jesus Christ our Lord,
who lives and reigns with you and the Holy Spirit,
one God, for ever and ever.

1 Samuel 2.1-10

Psalm 113

Romans 12.9-16b   *Luke 1.39-57*

℞

With a sense of urgency that increased almost by the day, she knew she had to get out. Even though it was still early in the pregnancy, her women friends particularly had an intuitive sense of these things that went beyond sight or speech. They would soon detect it, and then the questions would come—and worse, behind her back. She had seen it all with others many times in the village, the knowing smiles, the guesses, and then the slurs and insults, the public humiliation, even the danger to herself and the coming child.

She and Joseph had had their endless, desperate discussions. She had told him of her experience, to the degree that she could put it in words, and she had seen all too clearly the confusion of emotions reflected in his eyes. As he told her, trying to reassure her, he was aware of the idea of a birth such as she described. Galilee was a cosmopolitan area, well acquainted with the temples, myths, and rites of the Roman world. The birth stories of great figures of the Roman world were full of images of a young woman who walked in the woods or by the river and encountered a white bird from whom she learned of her pregnancy. One had only to walk the hour and a half journey north from Nazareth to Sepphoris to see the brilliant murals and be told the traditions about the maiden and the god. But it is very different to face such an event when it stops being myth and becomes part and parcel of your own life!

He had looked at her, his eyes full of love and pain, one chasing the other, one now stronger, now weaker. He had come to her a few days later and told her of his own dream, that in his troubled and exhausted sleep a messenger had come to reassure him that the child on the way was not a threat, but a glorious possibility. There remained one simple but all-important thing for Joseph to do. He was to wake, get up, go to Mary, and name the child. It did not matter that she had already been told that the child's name would be Jesus. Not until Joseph also named the child would he be able to accept fully what had happened. Not until he did this would the child be his also to love and care for. Joseph's dream speaks to every father. He must name the child, involve himself with its birth and nurture as it grows up.

Even with this reassurance, Mary knew only too well what they faced. The intimacy of village life could be supportive and reassuring in some circumstances, but it could also be harsh and unforgiving. All the reassuring conversations in the world with Joseph were not going to allow them to escape months of severe testing.

Years later she would tell Luke, as he interviewed her for the book he was writing, that she had left "with haste." Luke had smiled at her in his understanding way, but he hesitated over the obvious question about Joseph not going with her. The decision to go south to see her relation Elizabeth had been a spur-of-the-moment decision, and somehow, in a way she could not have said at the time, it had had nothing to do with men. It mattered not in the least that Joseph was with her in every way, that he fully accepted responsibility for what was ahead. When he assured her he understood, she knew that he meant it. It was just that he could not fully understand what it meant to be occupied by this other life at the very core of her being. She wanted—no, she needed—another woman to talk to, to confide in, to worry with, above all to understand. That was it, someone to understand. Who better than Elizabeth? She was not only pregnant herself, she was experiencing an utterly unexpected pregnancy, one that she had long given up hoping for.

There were moments on the long trek south when she doubted the wisdom of her decision. It had been difficult to get a place in a caravan as a single woman, but to travel alone was unthinkable. There was the long detour around Samaria that forced them to use the longer Jordan valley road, even though the home of her cousin Elizabeth and her husband Zachariah was south of the Samarian border, not far from Jerusalem, where Zachariah was involved in the endless round of the Temple worship. Instead of the comparatively easy journey along the pleasant valleys and vineyards of Samaria, she found herself dragging her increasingly tired body up the steep twisting road from the Jericho plain. As she toiled up the slope, she could not know that she would climb this same long steep grade as a young mother with her husband and her twelve-year-old son, anticipating their celebration of his coming of age, or that she would climb it in middle age, supported by her family and her son's circle of followers, knowing the horror that lay ahead of her.

Mary never forgot Elizabeth's welcome. "Blessed are you!" cried out the older woman, her face alight, her arms wide open. "Blessed are you and blessed is your baby!" She stood in front of Mary, making no effort to hide her own pregnancy, and for the first time, laughing and crying, Mary allowed herself to celebrate her own good news. Suddenly, to the surprise of both of them, she was singing as she clung to Elizabeth, crying out with her young voice a song that she had learned as a child, a song that Hannah had sung a thousand years before as she celebrated the pregnancy that would produce the child Samuel.

It was Elizabeth who collected herself first with words of mature and loving selflessness. "Who am I," Elizabeth cried, "that the mother of my Lord should come to me?" In that single sentence Elizabeth prefigures the relationship that will always exist between these two children. Time and time again in later years John will say of Jesus, "He must increase and I must decrease."

Mary's song comes to our ears as a song both lovely and terrifying. Other ages would come to know it as the *Magnificat*. In the monastic round of worship, it would become the song celebrating the approach of evening. It would become the center point around which the liturgical and musical jewel called evensong would revolve, yet it would also be a dark and terrible song of revolution. Why did she sing such a song that day? Was there something that told her the child within her was not only for her joy but also for her pain, was not only the lover of humanity but also the disturber of the world?

There is a sense in which Mary brings her unborn child to visit every one of us, asking from each of us the quality of welcome Elizabeth gave with such readiness and generosity. Mary brings herself and her son to each one of our homes, asking for the hospitality we can choose to give or to withhold. In this sense we are all Elizabeth, as she stands at her open doorway to watch the caravan passing on its way to the city. Through her eyes we are suddenly aware of a young, slight figure detaching herself from the long line of animals and people, waving goodbye to them, and then turning to pick her way up the rocky slope toward our waiting arms.

Saint Barnabas

Merciful God,
help us to follow the example of your faithful servant
  Barnabas,
who, seeking not his own renown
but the well-being of your Church,
gave generously of his life and substance
for the relief of the poor and the spread of the gospel;
through Jesus Christ our Lord,
who lives and reigns with you and the Holy Spirit,
one God, for ever and ever.

Isaiah 42.5-12 or Acts 11.19-30; 13.1-3
Psalm 112
Matthew 10.7-16

Ɒ

I saw him a number of times before realizing who he was—or perhaps I should say before he let me know who he was. Not only did he look exactly as I had always imagined he would look, he also spoke in the quiet way I had always assumed he would speak.

Every morning I go for a walk along the sea wall near my home. Recently I have been joined by a solid-looking man in his mid-fifties, with thin hair and a round, strong face. For a long time we did nothing more than salute in greeting as we passed, but one morning we met at the end of the wall where he was standing and looking out at some fishing trawlers. Then he said, as if to no one in particular, "Luke was kind enough never to mention that both Paul and I were seasick most of the time." We both burst out laughing.

"You're Barnabas of Antioch," I said as we shook hands.

"Yes," he answered. "Just before you came I was thinking that this little harbor is like the ones we used to go in and out of. Ships are different now, of course, at least the ones with engines. My God, how different it would have been for us if we had had one!"

"You went with Paul on that first journey," I said. "Why did you go?"

"Simple," he said. "Nobody else would."

"But why you? Was there some reason you couldn't say no?"

"Well," he said, "that's a long story. By the way, it's chilly here these mornings. Do you want to walk?" The two of us set off.

"I couldn't really refuse to go along with Paul, since I had got him to come to Antioch in the first place."

"Why Antioch?" I asked. "All of you seem to have headed there."

"Some of us went other places, to Phoenicia and Cyprus," Barnabas explained, "but the majority went to Antioch simply because it was big and cosmopolitan and we didn't stand out. You could disappear into the crowd in Antioch, and nobody cared what you believed as long as you kept reasonably quiet about it."

He paused a moment and then continued. "The trouble began when some of our people began to reach out to the Greeks instead of only to Jews. The Jerusalem community got alarmed and asked me to come up to Antioch and see what the situation was. Well, it turns out they sent the wrong man! I found those Greeks couldn't hear enough about our story—it excited them, and that excited me. After a few weeks I made the biggest decision of my life. I realized only one man could respond to this situation and that was Paul. Nobody I knew in Jerusalem had the brains for the job, although Stephen would have been a possibility if he had lived." He fell silent, but then his face brightened. "As soon as Paul came, things began to happen. We had a great response, so great that when news came from Jerusalem that the famine had hit there, our people collected huge amounts of aid and sent Paul and me south with it. I needed to go back to report anyway."

"Let me guess," I said. "You didn't tell them everything about the work among the Greeks and the Romans, not to mention the rest of the Gentile world?"

"Paul wanted to, but I persuaded him to keep his mouth shut. The whole thing came out later when we had done that first journey and the Jerusalem people called the Council together."

"So you both went back north to Antioch and then the idea of the journey came up?"

"Yes, and now you can see why I ended up as the traveling companion to one of the toughest, most singleminded characters in history! Paul made enemies as easily as anyone I ever knew—and not just Jewish ones. He even had enemies in our own community in Jerusalem. I spent half my life picking up the pieces after him."

"I've often thought about the fact that your name means 'son of consolation.' You've always been seen since as the one who picked up the pieces after Paul."

"Maybe that's true," Barnabas said, "but life is never that simple. Maybe there always have to be some pieces lying around because it's necessary to smash a few things. Paul was better at that than I. I realize now that it took someone like him to tackle the job. Those cities of Asia Minor were frontier towns. You had to be tough. There were a few times when it helped for me to calm Paul down and give a more temperate version of what he had said in some synagogue or other. I also had to shield Mark from the full force of Paul's temper; if he had known the contempt Paul had for him, I doubt he would ever have been part of the movement as long as he lived. Think what we—think what you—would have lost if that had happened! If I achieved nothing else, I did that. And even after Paul and I stopped working together, we stayed in touch. I guess I find it hard to cut people out of my life."

"It's your great gift," I said. "If you hadn't gone to Antioch and hadn't teamed up with Paul, if you both had not stuck to your guns about preaching to a bigger world than Judaism, I probably wouldn't be here as a Christian today."

"Maybe," he said, "but I think another way would have been found. I don't think the shock wave—isn't that how you say it?—of the resurrection could have been stopped. You see, it spoke with such power to a world that was dying. It transformed how people thought about the future. If we had not done what we did, I am quite sure another way would have been found."

"Is the gospel too powerful to be stopped at any time in history?" I asked.

He looked at me shrewdly. "I know why you ask that," he said. "I realize you people are having a hard time, and I know what the communities are going through right now. That is why you are asking, isn't it?"

"We don't have emperors or lions or anything like that. It's much more subtle. It has to do with the nature of belief itself. The whole world is asking the question Pilate asked back in your time, 'What is truth?'"

"I know," he said, "but it's not as different as you think. We had what you call pluralism and secularism, too. We had to match wits with some really brilliant, tough, Gentile minds. Paul saw this more clearly than anyone else. He was perfectly sure of resurrection, but he also knew that on the way to it stands a cross with a body on it. You people have to decide how toughminded and creative you are going to be to get through this time."

I looked at him as he stood there. He possessed both a gentleness and a strength; I could see it in the relaxed but firmly planted way in which he stood. It was in the muscles around his mouth and the lines around his eyes. It was in his eyes themselves. In his last sentence I had seen for a moment the steel beneath the velvet that made him what and who he was. He had come to say that last word to me.

I knew it was time to say goodbye. Barnabas could see it in my eyes. He put out his hand, smiled, and simply said, "God bless you." Then he turned and walked away along the sea wall.

11 June

The Birth of
Saint John
the Baptist

Almighty God,
you called John the Baptist
to give witness to the coming of your Son
and to prepare his way.
Give your people the wisdom to see your purpose,
and the openness to hear your will,
that we too may witness to Christ's coming
and so prepare his way;
through your Son Jesus Christ our Lord,
who lives and reigns with you and the Holy Spirit,
one God, now and for ever.

Isaiah 40.1-11
Psalm 85.7-13
Acts 13.14b-26   Luke 1.57-80

☙

Only in very recent years has it become possible,
standing in the southern end of the Jericho plain
and looking west, to see any sign of an urban
world. To the west the Jerusalem highway disappears into

the escarpment, and high on the brow of the rock stand the last houses and apartments of the settlement known as Maale Adumin. Even here you are still some miles from the actual city, but it is the first sign you have of city life.

I point this out because of something I have always suspected about the motives and actions of the extraordinary man whose life we remember on this particular day. We know him as John the Baptist, which is a kind of popular nickname to distinguish him from a thousand other Johns, a nickname given him because of something he invited people to do if they wished to associate with his movement.

John was a Nazirite, someone who withdrew from society to live a solitary and minimal existence. Such a stance and witness appears especially in times of turmoil and transition, as in the back-to-the-land movement of the 1960s in our own day. Where John differed from many who took that choice of solitary desert life in his own time, and where he differs from people making such choices today, is in his deep commitment to the society he had left. He was convinced that the world as he knew it was on the verge of massive change. He could only gropingly describe the terms in which he saw this change coming, but he was able to reach for an ancient image in his culture that he knew would be familiar to everyone. Change would come only from and through a person, someone who would be known as the Messiah.

Some of John's contemporaries thought the change would be political, advantageous to their country and its institutions. Others thought it would be in radical and desperately-needed social reforms, to use the language of our own time. High on the agenda of those who held this opinion was the matter of justice—social justice, as we would call it. John was in the latter camp, and from the gospel record it would seem he was already anticipating his cousin from the north, Jesus, as the Messiah to come. Certainly the fourth gospel hints at this possibility. Whatever the truth of this is, we do know that at a certain stage John came in from the desert and began a public ministry in the Jordan valley not far from where the highway to Amman crosses the river and the Jordan loses itself in the Dead Sea.

John decided to address his society in this harsh and rather lonely area rather than to go into Jerusalem itself, where he would have had a vast audience. I think this decision was of a piece with the rest of his attitude toward his society. He could have gone into the Temple area, as Jesus often did later, but he did not because he was not prepared to work within the existing structures. Today's equivalent might be the reluctance of someone like Alexander Solzhenitsyn to use the media as a way of getting through to the West. In his case the unhappiness and mistrust was mutual, but it gives us enough of an analogy to understand John's decision. Certainly Solzhenitsyn's message for the West and John's message for his time have much in common; for both of them, society lay under judgment, already condemned in their eyes—its customs and values, its public and private ethics, the huge abyss between rich and poor.

The wisdom of John the Baptist lay in his decision to force the urbanites of Jerusalem to come to him, rather than he to them. John knew well that countless voices had already preached what he wished to proclaim once again, for such jeremiads were familiar fare to the crowds in the Temple courtyards ever since the sixth-century prophet Jeremiah had given his name to the bringers of bad news. Instead, John began with those few people who happened to be in the southern reaches of the valley, trusting for word of mouth to reach westward to the city. Gradually the city folk began to come, and the groups turned to crowds, as he succeeded in getting the ear of his society.

If we take our place on the edge of one of his crowds, we hear that he is not merely shrieking condemnation of his generation and its world, but offering the blueprint for a better society, even though he addresses them harshly, calling them "a generation of vipers." He lures them into the desert so that they may for once look at their society from the outside and realize what a moral wasteland it has become.

John had the imagination to realize that something more than a nodding of heads was needed. That would do for long afternoons in the Temple area as one drifted from speaker to speaker; for John it was not enough. If there was truth in his intuition that a different kind of future was ahead, then a different kind of human being was needed for that future. That is why in baptism he invited people to take off their outer clothes as a symbol of self-revelation, to step into the shallow edge of the river, to trust themselves to strangers by falling backward into the water, disappearing from sight, and then struggling to their feet again. The action had many levels of very powerful meaning. By doing it you had first to step out from among others, itself a commitment, and then to forsake your dignity by removing your garments. You then had to go through a ritualized form of drowning. All in all it was a gesture of radical trust and commitment to John himself and to his vision of the future.

It is just at this point that John's greatness shows. He adamantly refuses to become the center of his own movement. At every opportunity he points beyond himself. There must have been many occasions when his inability to point to the agent of change brought sneers and contemptuous dismissal—was he no different from other ranters before him? And so it was until the day his cousin from Galilee stepped from the crowd, slipped off his outer robe, and asked John to baptize him.

Perhaps because of his premonitions, John was for a moment immobilized, freed only by the obvious calm of the eyes looking into his. In the next few moments he knew that his search was over. In the future there would be questions and doubts, but here on this day, standing in the shallows facing Jesus, there was only his certainty that the waiting was over.

Much more happened in the following months. John did not see it necessary to forsake his ministry; he may have even intensified his activities and accepted a higher degree of risk. Certainly he must have realized what he was doing when he challenged Herod's marriage to Herodias, the wife of Herod's brother, Philip. There followed weeks, even months, in the dungeons of Herod's Dead Sea fortress at Machaerus, from which there comes one more echo of John's voice before he is silenced forever by the executioner.

This moment is made all the more tragic by the fact that before his death John had sent a question through his followers to Jesus from prison, asking whether Jesus was indeed the Messiah, or if they should wait for another. The question shows clearly that he was wrestling with doubt about himself and his life's work. As soon as the messengers are gone Jesus turns to the crowd and, obviously struggling with his own emotions, says to them that among those born of women, no one is greater than John. One can only hope that some faithful friend found some means of passing this on to John before the axe fell.

Saint Peter &
Saint Paul

Almighty God,
your blessed apostles Peter and Paul
glorified you in their death as in their life.
Grant that your Church,
inspired by their teaching and example,
and made one by your Spirit,
may ever stand firm upon the one foundation,
Jesus Christ our Lord;
who lives and reigns with you and the Holy Spirit,
one God, now and for ever.

Ezekiel 34.11-16

Psalm 87

2 Timothy 4.1-8   *John 21.15-19*

❧

A s the two men wait in the quiet Jerusalem house for
their visitor to arrive, each is aware of the tension
they feel. It is not so much that they dread this
meeting—both of them have come through too much in recent years to be particularly disturbed by the prospect of a

difficult interview—yet they know how much hangs on it. They face a decision that will affect the lives of many others, and will decide the course of the community that trusts them and looks to them for guidance. Both Peter the apostle and James the brother of Jesus have much on their minds as they wait.

It is still very early in these tumultuous days of the birthing of the community, still the stage when nobody really knows what to do next. Various things have been set in motion, but in a rather haphazard way. Mark hasn't yet written his book; somebody whose name we may never know is gathering together the collection of Jesus' sayings we know only as Q. Communities are springing up here and there, and, as in all communities, the first resentments and disagreements are surfacing. Most people, at least in the Jerusalem area, still go instinctively to the Temple to take part in its worship. Danger is also beginning to appear with the resistance to the new Christian movement, including in recent years the obsessive hatred of a brilliant young lawyer from Tarsus with political clout.

Then unbelievable news arrives. Saul, the implacable enemy, it is said, has switched sides. Even as they wait for their visitor's arrival the two men discuss the news once more, searching it for inconsistencies, for the possibility that it is wish-fulfillment on the part of some Christians or, worse, that it is a political trap. Nothing has happened for the last few years, but the rumor about Saul of Tarsus persists and the campaign of hatred and violence has stopped. Nobody knows where Saul is, although it is said he has changed his name to Paul. Now he appears in Jerusalem, asking to meet Peter.

If we can trust the second-century writer Onesiphoros, the figure who entered the room that day and walked forward to meet Peter and James was not impressive. We have

Onesiphoros's detailed description of Paul: "A man rather small in size, bald-headed, bow-legged, with meeting eyebrows, and a large, red, and hooked nose." Was his unimpressive appearance an encouragement to the two leaders as they met this man who had been such a formidable opponent? Appearances aside, he was a brilliant scholar, sophisticated, with a mind like a razor. He was politically astute, at home in any society, with the social advantages of full Roman citizenship. Here was a combination to be handled very carefully.

Luke tells us that there was another person at that meeting. In his typically quiet, self-effacing, but courageous way, Barnabas had already met Paul in Syria and had made up his own mind about him. He had come to Jerusalem with his former enemy to make this meeting possible.

The introductions over, the questions began. It was probably not easy sailing. Luke suggests that the local communities still mistrusted Paul; as he puts it bluntly, "They did not believe that he was a disciple."

Whatever the outcome and however long it took to make the alliance, that was the first encounter of Peter and Paul, who were to become two of the great change agents in history. The relationship between them fascinates Christians for many reasons, not least because their differing gifts, personalities, and roles provide a pattern of contrasts that were to be important in the formation of the future church. These two were to have their moments of deep disagreement and confrontation. Given what we know of both of them—one a seasoned fisherman in the harsh environment of the lake, the other a seasoned debater in the cut and thrust of the Greco-Roman schools of rhetoric and law—we can imagine the intensity of their disagreement over eating with Gentiles! Who knows what went on between them as they hammered out their response to the challenges presented by the first council of Jerusalem? This must have been particularly difficult for Peter; unlike Paul, at this stage of his life he knew little or nothing about the vast reaches of the empire stretching away to the west. He had no idea, other than what he would have been able to gather from the life of Jerusalem, what it was like to live in that immense melting-pot of religions and lifestyles. Yet, at the end of the day, the instinctive conservatism of the one met the far-seeing vision and boundless energy of the other to rocket the news of their Lord from one end of that empire to the other.

The collect we use for their day points to the most valuable thing that happened between them, the factor that meant everything for the future. Immensely different, possessing very different visions of the future, they nevertheless battled their way to be "made one by your Spirit," in the words of the collect. If you stand in front of the National Cathedral in Washington, D.C., admiring the grace and power of that structure, this lesson is brought home to you. In front of the edifice the towers bear their names and carry their likenesses in stone. Together the foundations go deep into the rock of that hill and look out over a city where men and women wield a power undreamt of by that same imperial Rome where both Peter and Paul met their deaths.

We meet Peter in the gospel reading for today in his strong, self-confident early years. He has not yet left the lake for great affairs and responsibility; in fact, he has just fled back from Jerusalem. The horror of Jesus' execution is only weeks in the past. Peter has memories of his blustering in the upper room, his denial of any possible weakness, his later denial of Jesus himself. He meets Jesus with utter shame. What happens there on the beach in the dawn is one of the most moving episodes in all of scripture. In the single request, "Feed my sheep," repeated three times quietly and insistently, Jesus rescues Peter from his own shame.

The past is made irrelevant; in fact, it may be a wonderful preparation for future leadership. The fact that Peter now knows what it means to come apart at the seams as a human being makes him infinitely suitable for compassionate leadership, the leader par excellence for a tattered, stumbling community that has to be reassembled and led into an unknown future. One cannot help wondering if it was then that Peter realized that above all else the kingdom of which Jesus had often spoken was essentially about people: about caring for them, building them up, healing them, loving them. That would be Peter's great gift in the years ahead.

Life is never quite as simple as we want to have it, but it is possible to say that Peter's gift was the gift of the heart while Paul's was of the mind. Interestingly, the readings of this day do not so much emphasize the greatness of these two as their humanity and their vulnerability. In the epistle passage we catch a glimpse of a Paul who is old and tired, worn out by the impossible pace and demands he has always set for himself: "I have fought the good fight. I have finished the race. I have kept the faith." He may be tired and old, but that unyielding self-confidence is still there. Great saint Paul may be, but humility was never his strong point, not even at this late stage! The voice that we hear in the passage from the letter to Timothy—whoever held the pen that wrote it—is the voice of the teacher, the thinker, the formulator of a faith; in that sense it is the authentic voice of Paul. The person we meet by the hand of John the evangelist is in a sense shown to us naked, his humanity clearly revealed. We are less in the domain of the mind than of feelings. No one is being taught; someone is being healed. Both of these ministries have always been needed in the life of the church. It should come as no surprise to us that the needs of the church today are expressed over and over again as those of healing and teaching. Peter and Paul would understand those needs. Their work, their writings, and their lives have already given us insight and strength for them.

Saint Thomas

Almighty and everliving God,
who strengthened your apostle Thomas
with faith in the resurrection of your Son.
Strengthen us when we doubt,
and make us faithful disciples
of Jesus Christ our risen Lord;
who with you, O Father, and the Holy Spirit
lives and reigns eternally.

Habakkuk 2.1-4 or Hebrews 10.35–11.1
Psalm 126
John 20.24-29

☙

When you come up the great steps that bring you to Omar's magnificent Dome of the Rock, you turn to the right and walk east about fifty feet. There is no porchway here now, only the open plaza shrouded in a light fall of January snow. At this height, nearly four thousand feet above sea level, it is viciously cold and you have no difficulty identifying with Jesus as he searched for shelter to get out of the wind. "It was winter," John's gospel says cryptically. "The feast of the Dedication took place in Jerusalem, and Jesus was walking in the Portico of Solomon."

This morning, as I stand here in my fleece-lined jacket designed for the Canadian winter, I long for the shelter of that portico as I watch in my imagination this brutal day in Jesus' life. There is a crowd here today, as there was on that distant day, a crowd of pilgrims and tourists who are excited and curious. That crowd of long ago was threatening, querulous, volatile. "If you are the Messiah, tell us plainly!" a voice shouts. In reply, Jesus sounds weary and angry. "I have told you, and you do not believe." Within minutes things become ugly. As the crowd surges toward him, a group of Temple police try to get through to arrest him. Friends close swiftly around Jesus and someone finds a nearby door to safety.

Since it is impossible to stay in the area, Jesus' followers decide to travel south and east, over the ridge and down to the Jordan valley, across the river and into the foothills, where only a couple of years ago John began his baptizing ministry. Here they can be safe even if only for a while, and at least it will be warmer.

In the last few years Jesus has attained a high profile in a country where high profiles are dangerous, and it is essential that they all stay out of trouble. That means staying away from the Jerusalem area. It is precisely at this point that the news comes that none of them wish to hear. Lazarus, one of Jesus' closest friends, is ill.

For two days they do nothing, but then Jesus announces that he must go. His friends are appalled: "The Jews were just now trying to stone you, and you are going there again?" There is disbelief, anger, and fear in the question. Jesus is adamant. For the first time he tells them that Lazarus is dead. There is a stupefied silence, which for once is broken not by Peter, but by Thomas. His words are dogged and sulky, but they are words of absolute loyalty. "Let us also go, that we may die with him."

They make their preparations and head toward the river, the frigid wading through shallows, and then the long climb up to Bethany. If we walk with these men for a while we can watch them, assess them, see them in this strange situation each of them has chosen. If we do so, we realize one thing quite quickly. In spite of all the icons and paintings, they were not really a circle in the companionable sense we like to think. From the evidence of many incidents in the gospel narrative we know that the most intimate group around our Lord included Peter (but not Andrew, even though it was he who introduced Peter to Jesus) and the brothers, James and John. But as you would pick out a face in a group photograph, or as the camera sometimes zooms in on a face in a crowd scene in a movie, notice how there is a face always almost exactly in the middle of the group. He is never too far up front, never too far to the rear. It is the face of Thomas.

We are already learning something about him. It means something that Thomas is to be found somewhere in the middle, neither with Peter who leads nor with Judas who betrays. There are moments when he *does* lead, at least by taking the initiative, and at least one moment when, if he does not betray, he disassociates himself from a truth that all the others embrace. Thomas is in between, there but not there, believing but also leaving the door open.

So we begin to see who Thomas is—he is most of us in our spiritual lives. Most of the time we are more easily defined by who and what we are *not* than by who and what we *are*. Most of the time we are in between, showing up most of the time but not really committed to staying, believing in many things but keeping our options open. Thomas' face is familiar; it gazes out at us from countless reflections, in bathroom mirrors, in department store fitting rooms, in the rounded silver of a chalice, and sometimes, for a fleeting moment before we drink, in the smooth surface of the wine.

3 July

The Old Testament passage for his day from Habakkuk calls on the image of the watchman on the city walls, an image of absolute dependability. The watchman has to guard against delusions or visions; he must see clearly and decide about the nature of what he sees. The evidence of his senses is paramount because other people's lives depend on it. The passage from Hebrews speaks of endurance, of those who refuse to shrink back. This is exactly the Thomas with whom we are sharing the grim return to Jerusalem, his realism telling him at every step that they are walking into trouble, possibly even to their deaths. He is the same man who, months later at his final supper with Jesus, would ask, "Lord, we do not know where you are going. How can we know the way?"

Months go by. Jesus is arrested and crucified. Then, days later, the friend and leader they had seen die is reported to be alive. The disciples themselves are behind locked doors. Thomas leaves. We will never know the reason, but it is probably something quite ordinary: someone has to get supplies, keep families informed, and receive news for the beleaguered group. It would have been typical of Thomas' courage and practicality to have offered to take the risk.

At some moment during his absence the disciples experience the terrible beauty of Jesus' presence. "We have seen the Lord!" they shout at Thomas when he returns. Thomas looks at them, remembering the demoralized group he had left behind him. His stillness, his refusal to respond as they expect him to, brings a stunned silence. "Unless I see the mark of the nails in his hands, and put my finger in the mark of the nails and my hand in his side, I will not believe."

A week goes by. The disciples still gather from time to time for mutual support. Their lives have been turned upside down yet they have not the slightest idea what to do. Thomas is with them when Jesus appears to them a second time and when he is given, with infinite patience and understanding, his longed-for evidence. Being the kind of man he is, Thomas, who has withheld himself utterly, now gives himself utterly. On his knees this man of few and blunt words is entirely in character. "My Lord and my God!" Thomas blurts out.

We live in days that make Thomases out of many of us. These are not easy days for dreams and hopes. Our dreams of faith are painful, under assault in many ways. We spend much time behind locked doors of the spirit. May there be for us a sense of One risen and present. May we be given the power to cry out, "My Lord and my God," to kneel and to rise with our brother Thomas.

Saint Mary Magdalene

Almighty God,
whose Son restored Mary Magdalene
to health of mind and body,
and called her to be a witness to his resurrection,
forgive us and heal us by your grace,
that we may serve you in the power of his risen life;
who lives and reigns with you and the Holy Spirit,
one God, now and for ever.

Judith 9.1, 11-14 or 2 Corinthians 5.14-18
Psalm 42.1-7
John 20.1-3, 11-18

CR

T he turnoff to the *kibbutz* is by a gas station. After
that you are only a quarter of a mile or so from the
lakeshore, so you are soon in the parking lot. This is
one of the very few *kibbutzim* that is doing well financially
these days, and one of the things that has put it on the map
is the discovery a few years ago of a first-century fishing
boat. It was found entombed in the mud during a year when

the level of water in the lake was at its lowest for a long time. An international effort financed the task of rescuing the fragile timbers before the lake rose again, and today the boat lies in a huge tank just ahead of you, its timbers soaking in chemicals to ensure their preservation.

It could even be a boat that she had known, or one she sailed in at some time or other. It is intriguing to think of the possibility, because you are aware that you are very near her here. To the left, out beyond the parking lot in the long grass, if you were to dig deep down in the earth you would find the village of Magdala that she once knew and called home. Surely she played as a child on this shoreline, and as a young woman she often looked to the southwest in the evening to see the street torches being lit in what would have been to her the large, glamorous, sinful city of Tiberias. For us it is only a few miles down the road around the lake, but in her day the only way to Tiberias was by water, going across the dangerous part of the lake where she would have to pass the opening of the valley that leads west to Nazareth, down which the sudden, vicious winds blow from the distant Mediterranean.

We will never know whether she was aware early in her life that she was different from other children. Perhaps she would have forgotten the first terrible seizures if they had come in early childhood. It is only conjecture that epilepsy was the disease from which Jesus freed her; I suspect this is what Donatello had in mind when he carved her in wood in the fourteenth century. Her gaunt face bears a slightly distraught expression, the mouth drawn as if something inside is tearing at her. Her body looks strong and wiry, the muscles visible on her arms. She stands with her legs apart, one knee very slightly bent. Her arms and hands meet just below her throat, the fingers not quite touching. It is almost, but not quite, an attitude of prayer—she seems to be beseeching someone for something. Her hair is matted and long, reaching below her knees, a kind of wild, unkempt garment. The whole impression is of one immensely and passionately alive but living on the edge of nerves, the edge of nutrition, the edge of sanity. Did Donatello have in mind the appearance of the plague victims that would have been commonplace in his day in Europe?

Mary of Magdala has always possessed a kind of electricity about her in Christian memory, its collective imagination nourished by the ambiguities of the various gospel accounts, especially Luke's, of the unknown woman—legend associates her with Mary Magdalene—who anointed Jesus. With his usual vivid, narrative style, he takes us to the dinner party in the house of Simon the Pharisee. The supper would have been set in the increasingly fashionable Greco-Roman style that affluent Jews were adopting at the time, with guests lying on couches around the table. In the shadows of the surrounding colonnade it was permissible for the poor to gather, waiting for the occasional morsel or the chance to ask some favor of the rich.

Out of these shadows she comes, huddled down at the end of Jesus' couch. There she has access to his naked feet. One cannot do better than Luke for the sensuality of this moment: "She began to bathe his feet with her tears and to dry them with her hair. Then she continued kissing his feet and anointing them with the ointment." It is not difficult to imagine the camera angles, the muted lighting, the background music with which a movie director would produce the scene today. Its power lies not so much in its sexuality, but in the obvious passion that makes this woman oblivious to the way she invades this gathering. Fear of the rich and great does not exist for her. Something has freed her, and this freedom has given her the power to shatter the formality. She does this because she must, whatever the cost, and

the crowning beauty of this incident is that the one for
whom she does it understands, alone of all those around the
table, and accepts her utterly. If she is not yet a disciple of
this man, she most certainly will become one after this
night.

John's gospel narrates the moment in the garden when
Mary Magdalene comes upon the risen Jesus, face to face
with the man whom she does not at first recognize, and suggests that her first reaction is to hurl herself into his arms.
Jesus says, "Do not hold on to me." We have no way of re-
capturing his tone, but it cannot have been said in a way
that hurt or alienated her. When she goes from the spot and
links up with the disciples, the very simplicity of her statement communicates a serene, even joyful certainty. Mary,
the first person ever to have communicated with the risen
Lord, says simply, "I have seen the Lord." There is no suggestion of anything being held back; John says simply that
"she told them that he had said these things to her."

It is significant that the Mary we encounter in the terrible days of Jesus' passion is a very different kind of woman
from the one we meet at Simon's dinner party. The Mary
that has the courage to stand within sight of the crucifixion
of the man who obviously means everything to her is a
strong and courageous human being. The Mary that makes
her way to a tomb in the lonely hours of the early morning,
who will bring the news to the cringing followers in their
hiding place, has become a force in the community. She is
no longer the frantic, vulnerable figure carved by Donatello.

In the collect for her day we remember that Jesus "restored Mary Magdalene to health of mind and body." So
may he do for us if and when we should need such healing.
But at the same time the collect reminds us that he "called
her to be a witness of his resurrection." This is the insight
that her life sends to us across the centuries. Any healing

given to me is given for a purpose. It is given that I may then serve in some way the one who heals, that I may for the rest of my life, by the way I live, be a witness to his resurrection.

Today we pride ourselves on recovering a sense of the church as a healing community. Healing groups, pastoral teams, and mutual support groups flourish. The eucharist serves as the context of the laying on of hands with prayers for healing. All of this is something for which to thank God, but there are still two questions we must always ask about Christian healing. The first is, "What do I wish to be healed *from?*" The second is, "What do I wish to healed *for?*" Healing is not an end in itself, but the way to further service. We ask Jesus, "Let us be healed from our infirmities and know you." Mary of Magdala would have understood this. She experienced it.

Saint James

the Apostle

Almighty God,
we remember today your servant James,
the first apostle to give his life
for faith in Jesus Christ.
Pour out on all your people
that spirit of self-denying service
which is the mark of true leadership.
We ask this in the name of Jesus Christ the Lord,
who lives and reigns with you and the Holy Spirit,
one God, now and for ever.

Jeremiah 45.1-5 or Acts 11.27–12.3
Psalm 7.1-10
Matthew 20.20-28

CR

I had been asked to speak to a group of clergy who were on a morning walking tour in Jerusalem while doing a course at Saint George's, an Anglican college for continuing education. We were to meet in the Church of Saint Peter in Gallicantu, a lovely, ancient building just south of the old city of Jerusalem and outside the modern city walls.

I walked to the Damascus Gate and got into a taxi to go and meet them, but when I came down the steep sloping curve toward the church I learned that it would be a while before they arrived and I had some time on my hands.

Just outside the door of Saint Peter's there is a small refreshment room—just a few tables, some bottled drinks, and instant coffee. I went in there to cool off, sit down, and have some time to read. One other man was there already, about my own age, holding forth to the proprietor about his coffee. Not having the language, I could only guess that either it was not full enough or it was too strong or too weak; what impressed me was the vehemence of his protests. He had a great deep voice that thundered around the old stone arched walls. Whatever he was complaining about, he threw himself into it and eventually he got what he wanted.

As he came toward me on his way to a table he was still letting off steam, telling me of the low quality of the coffee and of those who served it, and of the general decline in everything these days. I realized he was not going to let me read in peace, so after he had hung around for a couple of minutes, obviously looking for companionship, I invited him to sit down.

The invitation transformed him. His voice became warm and friendly, his scowl was replaced by a smile. He extended his hand across the table and shook mine, saying in English, "Let's take our drinks outside. There is something I want to show you."

A little surprised, I followed him as he went out into the courtyard in front of the church's main door. We turned left and a walk of a few yards took us to a low wall over which we had a view down the hillside to the Kidron, across the Bethany road, and up the side of the Mount of Olives. He pointed out a long flight of shallow steps running down the hillside, slightly to our left and just below where we were standing.

"We often came up and down those steps," he said. "Back then they were the handiest way of moving through this part of the city. Actually, the night they took the Lord they brought him up those steps because the house of Caiaphas was here." He pointed down below us to the foundation area of Saint Peter's. "Later on, when you go down, you can see where they used to tie prisoners for interrogation."

It was a little like being in a dream. "Who are you?" I asked, although I thought I already knew.

"James," he replied. "Zebedee's son, John's brother. But that is less important than what I have to tell you." Brusquely he pointed down the hill sloping away in front of us.

"I want you to look again at the steps," he said. "Now look beyond them down there in the Kidron valley. See it?" I nodded. "Begin to move your eyes up the slope, just a little. Back then the whole slope of the hill was covered, mostly with olive trees. You can still see a few of them. Let me tell you about the last night. I have a theory about it I've never shared with anyone, not even with my brother John when he was writing about it.

"You remember how we left the upper room that night? Jesus seemed restless, like a trapped animal. The house was a bit further over there, on this slope." He pointed to the north. "We went down, into the Kidron. It's not a good place to be at night—unpleasant things can happen to you there. At a certain stage Jesus turned and gestured to all of us to stay where we were. Then he asked three of us—Peter, my brother John, and I—to come with him a bit further up the slope. We were already in the lower line of the trees, and we moved deeper in with him along a pathway that wound up the hill. After a little while he turned. I was terrified because he looked so unlike himself, distraught, as if out of control. He told us to lie down and rest, that he wanted to be alone.

"He was gone for awhile and we dozed. At one point one of the others went looking for him and found him in a small clearing, next to a large rock, clinging to it like a child. When he did come back—you know the rest—we were fast asleep."

He pointed again. "Look up toward the top of the mountain. Know what's over there?"

"Yes," I said. "Bethany."

"And after that?"

"You begin the long hike down to the Judean wilderness."

"That's the point," James said. "In those days if you went to the top of Olivet and headed east into the desert, nobody would ever find you again, not if you were young, healthy, and knew the area. He had all three going for him."

"What do you mean?" I asked, genuinely puzzled.

"I suspect that what was really going on that night was that he was trying to make the biggest decision of all," James said. "I suspect that's why he left the upper room. That's why he told us to stay at the edge of the trees. That's why he walked away even from the three of us and insisted on being alone."

"You think he was deciding whether to make a break for it or to stay and face it."

James looked at me. "Does that shock you?"

"No," I said. "Not a bit. It moves me deeply, and it brings him a lot nearer to me. It would be very human not to want to die at thirty, to want to run from the ordeal that he knew was in store for him if he stayed."

"I'm glad you feel that way," said James. "That's exactly what I feel, what I have always felt. I have never loved and admired him more than when I think of how much courage it must have taken to come back down the slope and rejoin us." He looked into the distance in a thoughtful sort of way.

"You know I let him down badly," he said. "Both of us did, John and I."

"How?" I asked. "I don't know of any terrible betrayal."

"That's it," he said. "It wasn't terrible, it was just a sleazy, mean thing that came over both of us. Mark put it in his gospel afterward; I guess Peter told him. We were on the way up from Jericho for the last time. All of us could feel in our bones this journey was different; we didn't know what was coming but we suspected it would change everything, whatever it was. Well, John and I had been with him for a few years at that point and we knew we had served him well. We figured it was on everybody's mind, so we decided to ask him right out to let us play a big part in whatever was coming.

"The minute we said it we regretted it bitterly, but it was too late. I could see the pain in his eyes. John was devastated at our miscalculation. I have never been so ashamed in my life. The irony was that every other member of the circle was doing the same kind of thinking and calculating. We were just the ones who made the mistake of saying it out loud."

He was silent, standing there leaning on the wall looking toward the Mount of Olives. The traffic was heavy at that time of day, nearing lunchtime. From where we stood we could see the never-ending tour buses parked outside the church. I realized I had better check if my group was ready for me.

"You have to go," he said, "and so should I."

There was something sad about him as he stood there, this strong, blustery man full of memories; as with most of us, guilt mingled with those memories. He was still there when I walked into the cool echoing vault of the church. The group was just ready for me and I preached the homily. When we emerged into the sunlight I looked to the right toward the low wall, but he had gone.

Saint Stephen

Grant us grace, O Lord,
that like Stephen we may learn to love even our enemies
and seek forgiveness for those who desire our hurt;
through your Son Jesus Christ our Lord,
who lives and reigns with you and the Holy Spirit,
one God now and for ever.

Jeremiah 26.1-9, 12-15   *Acts 6.8–7.2a, 51c-60*
Psalm 31.1-7, 16
Matthew 23.34-39

☙

I t is almost impossible to park here. The bus grinds to a
halt halfway down the hilly street and the driver begs
everyone to get out as quickly as possible amid the
beeping of horns in protest. Before us the hill rises toward
the city wall and the gate. It has had many names, but one
of them is his. This is Saint Stephen's Gate. If you turn to
the east and look over the Kidron Valley, you will see the Orthodox oratory that also bears his name. Somewhere
nearby—probably down on the floor of the valley because
they liked to keep public executions outside the bounds of
the city—he was killed.

There is a famous painting of Stephen's stoning by the Italian painter Giulio Romano. In the foreground is the kneeling figure of Stephen, and what strikes you first is how young he looks. Behind him in a semicircle are his tormentors; behind them, stretching into a "heart of darkness," a river flows away into a medieval landscape. At one end of the semicircle is another very youthful figure whom we recognize with a shock as Saul, sitting among the garments of the executioners, so near to Stephen that their outstretched hands almost touch. Above them a great bank of dark clouds is crowned by God the Father and Christ the Son, gazing down with expressions of deep pity, the arm of the Christ raised as if in salutation or welcome.

I was just about to turn away from the view of the Kidron and move into the alleys of the old city when I heard a voice. It was young, confident, and a bit sarcastic.

"The problem with Luke's book is that in trying to make me into a shining idealist, he also makes me sound like a fool."

The voice cut through my thoughts, startling me. He was standing a few yards away leaning against the corner of the gate, looking like most of the other young men around in jeans, shirt, mustache, thick black hair.

"So you did realize right from the beginning what you were getting into?" I asked Stephen.

"Of course I did!" he said sharply. "I would have been crazy not to."

"Why did you get involved with the movement at all?"

"I was looking for something, and the people I met seemed to have found something to live for. That was important to many of us then. You see, there was a feeling around that nothing was ever going to change as long as Rome stayed in power. What Jesus gave us was another reason for being alive, the possibility of forming a new kind of society."

Something about his tone, the hint of his voice just trailing off, made me look around. I spotted a few outdoor tables and said, "Why don't we have some coffee?"

"The first thing that happened after I joined," said Stephen after we were settled, "was that an ugly fight broke out between two factions in the movement. I should have seen something right then but I didn't, probably because I didn't want to. They had taken on responsibility for a great many women who had been widowed; widows were vulnerable and it's to the credit of the movement that every day a decent meal was provided for any who came. It was also a way of recruiting followers, I guess, but that wasn't the main reason."

I kept quiet and he went on. "The problem was that some of the women were Hebrew-speaking and some Greek. That meant trouble because the rift was far more than language; it turned out they were worlds apart, and I should really have known it because of my own upbringing. You see, what most people don't realize is that Judaism at that time was an immensely varied phenomenon with countless schools of thought. Many Jews saw nothing strange about following Jesus as a Jewish teacher while continuing their faithful and lifelong worship in the Temple. Most of these people had lived all their lives in Jerusalem; it was the whole world to them. But there was another part of the movement composed of very different people. Their world was much larger. Most of them had traveled. Most of them spoke Greek and a couple of other languages, including Hebrew. But the difference was in the way these people felt themselves to be part of the empire and its institutions, particularly the Greek traditions and Greek culture that were at its heart."

"That's the world you yourself were brought up in, wasn't it?" I asked.

He nodded. "Yes—and, ironically, that is what made people like me attractive to some of the leaders of the movement. They hadn't yet done much about it, but some of them suspected that Jesus was bigger than Judaism, and therefore there was a bigger future ahead. They didn't know how—that wouldn't come until Paul—but they suspected."

"One thing puzzles me," I said. "I still don't see why things went the way they did, right up to their actual killing you. Surely the rift wasn't that deep?"

"Depends on your point of view. Don't forget the other part of the story—Rome. The authorities knew they were sitting on an extremely explosive situation and they said a number of times that if there was any more social unrest, dire consequences would follow. So there we were, a movement making a lot of noise that seemed to be about radical social change. At some stage the decision must have been made to watch us very carefully. We knew that, of course. We weren't fools."

"Is this when Saul appeared on the scene?" I asked.

"Not in any obvious way," Stephen replied, "but he was probably involved in surveillance from the start. We had heard about him; after all, Jerusalem was pretty small. When he and I did meet at my so-called trial, I realized that I had seen him around on some occasions when I was speaking to groups."

"The trial," I said. "Why did that go the way it did? How was it possible to get a death sentence passed, considering that you were really only a *potential* threat? You hadn't *done* anything."

"Yes, I had," he said quickly, sharply. "It's difficult for you to see it, but I had. I had given the impression that I and others like me wanted to do away with the whole system of

Judaism, or at least to change it radically. To use the language of that time, I was out to destroy the Temple."

"Is that why people from your own movement testified against you?"

"Of course," he said bitterly. "Remember I told you of that rift between the Greek and Hebrew elements among us? When push came to shove the latter group stayed with the Temple system, and its preservation became more important than the common loyalty to Jesus. That was the real shock for me and that was the one thing I didn't take into account. Of course I know now that the Hebrew congregation in Jerusalem became just a historical footnote, but how were we to know that the Romans would destroy the city and the Temple and explode the whole thing across the eastern Mediterranean?"

"What about Saul? What about his change of heart?"

Stephen looked away, thought for a bit. "I don't know. I remember the way our eyes would lock at some points in the trial. I had the feeling I meant a lot to him. At that time I thought it was only in terms of really wanting to get me as a warning to the whole movement. But I wonder if there wasn't more to it. Looking back, I think now there was some kind of affinity between us. God knows, we were both totally singleminded." He suddenly grinned ironically. "Maybe conflicting fanaticisms form a bond between the people crazy enough to hold them!"

I could tell he was getting ready to leave. "Do you really mean what you just said?" I asked. Pushing the small table back, he replied, "Perhaps not quite like that. But if you're asking me if I think what happened to me was the reason for Paul's change, the answer is yes, I do. At least—put it this way—I hope it was the reason." He got up and walked over to the low wall from where you could see the Kidron. He stood for a moment, looking down, then said quietly, as if talking to himself, "If it was, it makes what happened down there worthwhile."

Without turning back to look at me or to say goodbye, he walked quickly away.

The
Transfiguration
of the Lord

Almighty God,
on the holy mount you revealed to chosen witnesses
your well-beloved Son, wonderfully transfigured:
mercifully deliver us from the darkness of this world,
and change us into his likeness from glory to glory;
through Jesus Christ our Lord
who lives and reigns with you and the Holy Spirit,
one God, now and for ever.

Daniel 7.9-10, 13-14
Psalm 99
2 Peter 1.16-19   Luke 9.28-36

&

In the parking lot at the foot of this mountain the
stretch limousines are lined up waiting for business,
their engines humming. Each will take seven people, all
chatting to each other nervously as they climb in, because
someone who has taken this trip already has hinted to them

of the thrills to come. The moment the last door has closed
the driver takes off, his goal to impress, not merely to trans-
port. At least one driver lets out a loud "Alleluia!" as he
changes the first succession of gears. It is one of the very
few words he knows that will be understood by his passengers.

The road up the mountain is narrow, rough, and winding,
full of hairpin turns. At no time is there a guard rail or anything else to prevent the taxi becoming, for a few short moments, a glider. At each bend there are ever more
magnificent views of the valley of Jezreel. Now and then two
taxi drivers delight in meeting one another coming from op-
posite directions, a situation in which somebody has to
swerve as far out as possible; then you close your eyes and
remind yourself that you are on a religious pilgrimage.
Surely God would not allow a pilgrim to go over the edge!
At some rational level in your mind you know that generations of pilgrims before you all down the centuries have said
similar prayers and yet never saw home again. You resolutely
cast this thought from your mind, and suddenly, as you do,
you are at the end of a long, narrow, but—thank God—level
driveway. You sweep through an ancient archway into the
courtyard of the Franciscan basilica that crowns Mount Tabor.

We have come here because in this place one of the great
and beautiful mysteries at the heart of Christian faith took
place. If we look to the north and slightly east we see the
snow-crowned slopes of Mount Hermon, and some legends
claim that it was on those slopes that Jesus was transfigured
in the company of his disciples. A stronger tradition argues
for the spot where you are standing, at the summit of
Mount Tabor, about half a dozen miles from Nazareth at the
southern flank of what is today called Upper Galilee. Either
way, we could not have come to a better vantage point to

see a vast panorama of this part of the world that Jesus knew and loved as his home.

We walk away from the entrance to the basilica, leaving the courtyard in front of it, and then turn left to a narrow path that takes us into a wooded area that looks away to the south. Most of those who come up Tabor are not aware of this quiet place. We sit and think about the event that took place here long ago, and perhaps find out at least some of the truths about our own lives that it may reveal.

Did he know what would take place up here in this clear air under this blue sky? I have been here also when the sky was dark and the winter clouds moved swiftly before the wind. Did he know? Or did he come because it was one of those times for him to get out from under the constant demands and pressures of the public life he had chosen? We are tempted to think he knew everything, that tomorrow was as much a known quantity for him as yesterday is for us. We long for that kind of knowledge. But we need to remind ourselves that if it is true that Jesus came among us to taste fully our human limitations, then tomorrow for him must always have been as much a mystery as it is for us—sometimes longed for, sometimes dreaded, but always a mystery, a not-yet, a possibility not yet real.

You wonder which one of the three who went with him related the events of that day. Mark tells us of it in his book, so it is likely the story came from Peter. If so, that honest man does not attempt to make himself sound better or wiser than he really was, a trait that endears him to us even more.

Here on Tabor there is a natural exhilaration that is hard to describe. The air is thinner, the light constantly changing, and in certain seasons a mist falls suddenly and lifts again quickly. If you decide to forego the taxi for the forty-five-minute climb, you arrive with pounding heart and throbbing blood, tired but intensely alive. That is how they may have felt, throwing themselves down somewhere within earshot of where we sit at this moment. Sometime soon afterward—a minute, an hour, half a day later—everything changed for the four of them forever. We do not know how it changed Jesus, but we know that it changed the relationship between him and the three friends who witnessed what happened and who later tried so hard to tell the story accurately.

I can hear Peter very clearly as he tries to tell the story years later to Mark. I can see Mark's listening face, eyes focused on the older man, hand poised over the writing surface. I can see flashes of slight impatience as Peter struggles to make sense of it, remembering his babbling on that day and now determined not to babble again, but to be clear and concise.

First the memory of the clothes, blazing white, instilling sheer terror. There is no terror like that of the utterly familiar suddenly changing in front of us, revealing things we have never guessed at. Then the realization that they were no longer alone on the mountain, that they were witnessing some kind of visitation across time and space. Was it an offering of images and pictures by which they could begin to understand what they had got themselves into with this friend from Nazareth? Whatever the truth, Peter tells of the presence of Moses and Elijah. He remembers that his friend is conversing with these figures who, had Peter been Greek or Roman, he would have thought of as gods.

All three of them are utterly outside what is happening, wondering spectators looking through a window between the worlds, children with their noses pressed flat against the glass, eyes wide, mouths open with awe. They do not know what to say, so, as usual, Peter says it. A wish to be helpful, to do something, anything, comes out in words tumbling one over the other. He will build something that will enshrine this moment, this experience unlike anything he has ever known. He searches for a way to grasp and hold this glory and terror and ecstasy.

And then the cloud comes, sweeping in over the mountain, as this one far above us could engulf us today if we stayed here long enough. The cloud comes as a blessing. It takes the blinding light from your eyes. It allows you to recover some sense of self, some semblance of control. And then the voice speaking within your mind, the coming of utter certainty that the friend with whom you climbed this mountain is far more than any friend, is a reality and a mystery for which no language exists.

"Suddenly when they looked around," writes Mark, "they saw no one with them any more, but only Jesus." Luke differs only slightly in what he writes. Again there is the sense of a great stage that was once full and is now empty, echoing: "Jesus," writes Luke, "was found alone." He also adds an interesting postscript: "They kept silent and in those days told no one any of the things they had seen."

We find it no less difficult to share our experiences of the presence of our Lord. The more intense and transfiguring our experiences on the mountain, the more wary we are of revealing them to others. Peter and James and John are no different merely because they are human beings of another time; years will go by before Peter risks sharing this day. Its grace will kindle within him and within the other two and will take them through the days to come, the days of Jesus' arrest, trial, and execution. In the days of resurrection they will remember this light because they will see it again. In the long years ahead, years requiring mundane, unrelenting faithfulness to many tasks, this day will sustain them.

Our approach to the transfiguration will be different for each one of us. Some of us will sit on this hillside and literally recapture it; others will hear of it through scripture. But whether we are able to walk this mountain or merely to see it through the eyes and ears of witnesses, most important of all is our willingness to search for those moments when something in our experience is lit by a light beyond ourselves. It can be in our experiences of beauty, of nature, of sex, of worship, of prayer. There is no end to the doors by which the wind and the light and the voices of transfiguration can enter our lives.

Like Peter, we will want to grasp and hold the moment. As on that day, the experience will be followed by a cloud, a kind of sadness at losing something. But if we listen, there can be a voice in the cloud, and when it lifts, we will be aware that our Lord is present. We will, even if only for a moment, have been given the gift of "beholding the King in his beauty." If we resent the fact that it can be only for a moment, we can comfort ourselves with the realization that we can look at such beauty for no more than a moment. If it were ours for longer, we would not be able to bear it.

Saint Mary
the Virgin

O God,
you have taken to yourself the blessed Virgin Mary,
mother of your incarnate Son.
May we who have been redeemed by his blood,
share with her the glory of your eternal kingdom;
through Jesus Christ our Lord,
who lives and reigns with you and the Holy Spirit,
one God, now and for ever.

Isaiah 7.10-15
Psalm 132.6-10, 13-14   *Galatians 4.4-7*
Luke 1.46-55 or Luke 2.1-7

❧

W hen I was a small boy in the 1930s growing up in
the south of Ireland, we had what was called in
those days a "maid" to do the housework. She was
not responsible for looking after us children, but I can recall
a long rainy winter afternoon about the time I was five when
she was either reading to me or telling me a story. For some
reason the talk veered into things religious and she told me

the story of the Blessed Virgin Mary. In terms of those long-ago days in the south of Ireland, the good lady probably thought of herself as doing missionary work among these poor Protestant children who had good parents and a nice home but, alas, did not have the Catholic faith.

She must have told the story well because everything about the experience has remained vivid after sixty years. She told me of how beautiful the Virgin Mary was, and she showed me a medallion that was hanging around her own neck and that carried the likeness of the Virgin. She then told me about the Virgin Mary living for some years in the house of Saint John until one day angels came to the house, surrounded it, lifted it into the air, and carried it across land and sea until they reached Loreto in Italy, where they put the house back down.

As you can imagine, this in itself was an exciting story for a child, but it continued. When the Virgin was an old woman and near death, the angels came again. This time they surrounded her and took her with them into the heavens. Those who were watching could see that the Virgin Mary was no longer old and sick, but had become as beautiful as she had been in her youth. Ever after, she is with her son Jesus in heaven, near the throne of God, where she often intercedes with the Father and her son Jesus for people who pray to her and need her help.

You will know from your own childhood how real that story was for me. Some years later, when I was at college, the pope promulgated the doctrine of the Assumption of the Blessed Virgin Mary and it became an integral part of the Catholic faith. In some sense it is true to say that at least for me it had already become an integral part of Christian faith at the deeper levels of the imagination.

The trigger for that memory was the opening statement of the collect for Saint Mary the Virgin's day. We say something unique about her that echoes that old story: "God, you have taken to yourself the blessed Virgin Mary." It is a tribute to the storytelling gift of our housekeeper that even today I tend to give that phrase a very precise meaning; I see the Virgin borne aloft by shining ones, herself shining, ethereal, beautiful, and (such are the fantasies of childhood) interceding for me among all those formidable male figures on and around the throne of God. When I read the passage from Isaiah that we use for her day, I am intrigued that the images of the passage—"clothed with the garments of salvation...covered with the robe of righteousness...a bride adorned with her jewels"—all fit in with my childhood memory of her being swept aloft in a wonderful way.

That is a vivid memory of my childhood, but I also have a most moving experience to share as an adult of a moment spent in Nazareth, where she once lived and brought up her family. The Convent of the Sisters of Nazareth stands in what is today the bustling downtown of Nazareth, located up a narrow lane from which, when the bell is answered, you are let in to a quiet and lovely courtyard. Not very many people come here, other than those who stay as guests in the wing allotted for that purpose, and groups who come as students from various schools across the country.

In the late nineteenth century, when Nazareth was still a very small town, the Roman Catholic bishop of this area invited an order of nuns from France to establish a house. The first thing they had to do was to buy a piece of land in Nazareth. They selected a plot on a hill at one end of the town; then they did the expected bargaining, and eventually bought it and began to build. In the course of construction the Mother Superior was approached by an elderly man who said to her, "I suppose you know that you have bought the house of the Just Man?" The Mother Superior became wary, suspecting that the price was about to go up for this mysterious and cryptic reason. But her suspicions were groundless. The man merely wished to tell her that ever since anyone in the area could remember, the piece of land on the hillside had been said to be the site of the house of the Just Man. Tantalizingly, the Just Man was never given a name.

Years went by and the legend of the Just Man became part of the story of the convent. It was not until many decades later that some workmen were excavating the foundation in order to make room for an extension of the buildings, and they broke through to discover a flight of steps leading to what later was authenticated as a first-century house.

I went down those steps with some others who, like me, were not yet aware of the tradition of the Just Man. We had not yet been told the story I have related here. It was not until we were standing in the house itself that we heard it. I was deeply touched. Neither I nor anyone else immediately leapt to the conclusion that this was the house of the holy family, although it was certainly from the right period. Much of the house is still intact, and the walls stand as they once did. At one point it is obvious that the Crusaders built an arch over this place, another indication that they too in their time were told that there was some special significance about this place.

To stand in the doorway of the house is particularly moving. As you pause between its stone sides, you know that others long ago stood here and looked out. Even if this house is not that of Joseph the carpenter and his wife Mary, we can imagine the possibility that in the coming and going of village life, one or other of them may have entered this doorway for some neighborly purpose. As you stand in this doorway, now deep beneath the earth, you know that someone stood here and looked down the village street at children playing, among them a boy shouting and leaping and laughing with the rest. I found it difficult to step back from the doorway and let someone else take my place.

Memories and experiences: both are part of my relation-ship with people from long ago, especially with one woman who is now a great icon at the heart of Christian faith. The story told me in childhood left the impression of a beautiful young woman; my visit to Nazareth as an adult gave me a sense of her presence as wife and mother. Neither of these experiences can by their nature be more than a dream, but they have been very powerful and lasting dreams. They are the means whereby the Blessed Virgin Mary is more than a religious figure, more than a character in the Bible, more than a line in the rhythms of the creed. By such experiences she has become for me a reality, a person, a companion, a woman.

Saint Bartholomew

Almighty and everlasting God,
who gave to your apostle Bartholomew
grace to believe and preach your word,
may your Church truly love what he believed
and faithfully preach what he taught;
through Jesus Christ our Lord,
who lives and reigns with you and the Holy Spirit,
one God, now and for ever.

Deuteronomy 18.15-18 or 1 Corinthians 4.9-15
Psalm 91
Luke 22.24-30

❦

The more I come to know about the people Jesus chose to be his disciples, the clearer it is that he did not choose them for any spectacular qualities. Take Bartholomew, for instance, who is a very ordinary, decent man, pleasant to meet. To this day he is astonished to find himself a household word, his face captured forever—a bad likeness, he insists—by Leonardo da Vinci at the Last Supper.

"Why is it," he asked me in an exasperated voice, "that we all look so chronically serious in these great paintings, as you call them? I have never seen anything but a kind of melancholy seriousness on our faces. Doesn't anyone realize that we laughed a lot? God knows we certainly argued a lot. Nobody would ever think it to look at us in your canvasses and mosaics and frescoes and whatever else you have frozen us all into. We even danced sometimes. I get the feeling that if any of you Christians saw us dancing around a campfire, you would really worry about what you like to call the early church!"

I first met Bartholomew when I was traveling around Galilee for about a week. That morning we had been out at the coast at Acco; later, when I told Bartholomew about the trip, he reminded me that in his time it was called Ptolemais. As a child, he said, he had always been proud of the fact that there was some connection with the name of that city and his own family name, Bartholomew. He wasn't sure why Mark had used his family name in the list of the disciples, but he was glad John got it right some years later when he called him Nathanael in his book.

During our morning in Acco we heard a lecture about the period of the Crusades and after lunch we set off inland for the higher country to the east, reaching Cana by early afternoon. Naturally Nathanael was on my mind, since John's gospel tells us he had come from here and at one point the guide reminded us of that, adding that Cana was his own town. When not a tour guide, he taught school here. The nice thing about being in Galilee with our group for a week was that he got to go home each night to his family. In Cana we did what all visitors do, which is to walk up the narrow, high-walled street to the little Franciscan church, listen to a scripture reading, dutifully look at the replicas of stone jars that stand in the crypt, then go across the road and purchase a bottle of the not-so-wonderful local wine. By now it was late afternoon and the guide suggested we might have a little time on our own. He and I were standing near each other as the others moved away, so he invited me for coffee—he knew a pleasant spot a block or two away, a cousin's place.

When we were seated, he said very simply, "I am Nathanael, and it is very good to meet you here in my city." I couldn't hide my confusion—this man? He seemed so rooted here in the present. "Yes," he said, "I really do teach school here and I really do manage to fit in some tour groups from time to time, but, in a way that I can't explain to you, I am also Nathanael.

"Do you want to know how it all began for me?" he asked. "I know John has said a little, but it might interest you to hear it first-hand. I was very young when I first met Jesus—we all were. It seemed to be a generational thing, which is why many older people, including my parents, were so worried about us. Anyway, some of us were involved in a movement led by John Bar Zachariah, who was convinced we were all on the edge of enormous renewal and change and we had to be ready for it. When people were ready to commit themselves, he took them into the shallow water of the Jordan and held their heads under the water for a moment, to show that they had died and were born again as a different person.

"A friend of mine—his name was Philip—had gone south, he and a few others. They were all from the north shore of the lake, over by Bethsaida. It was while they were down south they met Jesus. I don't know what took place on the long journey north, but by the time they got back to the Galilee Philip was convinced beyond a shadow of doubt that Jesus was what we had always hoped for, the one who was going to make all the difference. He didn't even wait to go back to Bethsaida, but persuaded the whole group to detour north through here."

"Speaking of Jesus," I said, "you still haven't told me how you met."

"No, I haven't," he said. "You passed through Nazareth on this tour the other day, didn't you? It's huge today, two cities in one, Arab and Jewish, traffic near gridlock, air unbreathable. It's much bigger than Cana. But you should have seen Nazareth in my time—a hick town! I tried to get out of going but Philip kept at me. In the end I gave in and went."

He paused as though searching for a way to go on. "Do you want more coffee?" he asked. I shook my head. I didn't want him diverted at this point.

"Philip knew I was about to give in—he always knew the moment to close in! Before I knew it we were on our way together."

Nathanael pointed across the valley, across the roofs of the suburban homes along its side. His voice became quiet, less assured, less flippant. "It was over there, on that hillside. The group of them had come up from the south and were on their way home. Andrew was there, and Simon. Naturally at that stage I didn't know any of them, but I remember how I barely noticed them. I was aware only of meeting him—there was something about him. He never made you think he was trying to be anything or anybody else. I guess that's it. He was truly himself in a way I had never seen before.

"First thing he said to me was a joke, something like, 'Well, here comes one of the few honest men in Israel!' I didn't know what to say because I hadn't expected him to be bluff and hearty like that. So I said to him, 'How did you hear about me, anyway?' He laughed and pointed back over the valley. 'We could see Philip working on you over there. We could see you coming from the moment he got you up from under that fig tree of yours.'

"Something strange happened then, something inside me. It didn't come from what he had said—we were just kidding around. It was from the simple fact of being in his presence. Have you had moments in your life when suddenly you know that this moment has come and it will never come again if you live to be a thousand years old? You have to say yes to it with your whole heart, and you hear a voice saying it as if from very far away and the voice is your own voice, and the yes is coming from you?"

Both of us were silent. I began to think of all the things we had not talked about, such as what had happened to Nathanael himself after the Lord had risen. Had he really gone to India, as tradition says he did? What about Armenia, where tradition says he died? I knew all these things would have to wait. Maybe there would never be another time, but somehow that did not seem to matter.

He knew what I was thinking. "No, we can't talk about the other things," he said. "What we did talk about is the important part: how each of us meets him and when each of us says our yes to him."

He looked at his watch. "I told them the bus would be at the end of the block at 4:30. We should go." For a moment, as we headed out, he put his arm around my shoulders.

"How did John put it? 'An Israelite in whom there is no guile.' Not bad." He looked into my eyes and smiled. "Good to have met." In the parking lot the first of the early birds were already gathered around the bus, souvenirs and purchases firmly in hand.

The Beheading of John the Baptist

Almighty God,
who called John the Baptist
to give witness to the coming of your Son
and to prepare his way,
strengthen us by your grace,
that as he suffered for the truth,
so we may boldly resist corruption and sin,
and receive with him the unfading crown of glory;
through Jesus Christ our Lord,
who lives and reigns with you and the Holy Spirit,
one God, now and for ever.

2 Chronicles 24:17-21 or Hebrews 11:32-40
Psalm 71.1-6, 15-17   Mark 6:17-29

℞

Perhaps a good measure of John's true place in the pantheon of Saints in the Prayer Book is the fact that he is one of three figures who are given more than one day. Only Peter and the Blessed Virgin Mary — she

alone is given three — share with John the distinction of re-
ceiving more than one celebration.

Another measure of John's true worth is the obvious af-
fection and respect our Lord had for him. Their relationship
could not help being ambiguous. The movement John had
begun was winding down as Jesus came on the scene. One
of the very sad moments in the New Testament is described
by John the Evangelist in the early part of his gospel. John
the baptizer, as he was nicknamed, is chatting to two young
men who have been part of his movement. As they talk,
Jesus of Nazareth passes by. John points him out to his two
followers and readily affirms what Jesus is doing. Bringing
the conversation with John to a close, the two move away
from him and begin to follow in the direction that Jesus has
gone. Eventually they become followers of Jesus and the
new movement.

This must have happened on more than one occasion, yet
there is never the slightest indication that John showed any
resentment. Again and again John admits that he sees himself as nothing more than the herald of a greater leader, a
preparer of the way. To do this consistently and without any
sign of bitterness is the mark of real greatness, a greatness
that Jesus mentions more than once and for which he had
immense respect.

Although both John and Jesus were instigators of religious
movements in their country at much the same time, there
were profound differences between them. It is obvious that
John was prepared to be confrontational in the extreme. To
address one's audience as a "brood of vipers" is hardly con-
ducive to one's popularity as a reformer! Nothing we hear
from John shows any similarity to Jesus' narrative style.
John's primary objective seems to be to attack patterns of
personal immorality in the society. He tells soldiers to re-
frain from demanding protection money from people. He

tells tax gatherers to be reasonable in their demands. John is even prepared to condemn the personal behaviour of Herod himself, the local ruler, attacking the morality of his marriage.

The gospel writers hint at a subtle and ambiguous relationship between Herod and the troublesome prophet in his kingdom. Luke suggests in his gospel that John more than once attacked Herod's actions and policies. Yet for some reason Herod was prepared to take this from John. Mark tells us that when Herod heard John "he was greatly perplexed, and yet he liked to listen to him." There was a long tradition in Israel of the legitimacy of a prophet challenging the ruler. The classic case was Nathan's courageous condemning of David for his betrayal and murder of Uriah, whose wife David had seduced. Even when Herod does take action against John, arresting him and imprisoning him, Mark takes care to say that Herod did this "on account of Herodias, his brother Philip's wife, because Herod had married her ... Herodias had a grudge against John and wanted to kill him." On the other hand, says Mark, "Herod feared John, knowing that he was a righteous and holy man, and he protected him."

However that protection was not enough. In a story that has since formed the basis of oratorios and operas, Herodias engineers Herod into a position where he cannot save John without appearing to break his own word. A measure of the guilt that Herod must have felt is shown in his response, some time later, when he hears about the success of the new movement begun by Jesus of Nazareth. He immediately fears that John has been raised from the dead. We cannot help but notice the self-accusing phrase, *"John, whom I beheaded..."*

John's work is more a reform movement than a social revolution. He claims no overall vision of a transformed human nature. He is convinced that some agent of great change is about to affect his society, but he does not profess to know how. To prepare for this event, he deals in efforts to change specific human behaviour. There is nothing in John to parallel our Lord's vision of the kingdom of God or the kingdom of heaven — a vision in which all human values are turned upside down by the values of a kingdom where the weak are strong, the first last, and the poor wealthy. Yet when we have said all this, we cannot dismiss the significance of the tribute paid to John by our Lord's decision to come to him at the Jordan and to accept baptism. Obviously there is no wish on the part of Jesus to dissociate himself in any way from John's work.

At the height of Jesus' ministry, when great crowds were gathering to hear him and, as Luke says, "word about him spread throughout Judea and all the surrounding country- side," something extraordinarily moving takes place in the relationship of Jesus and John.

The fortress of Machaerus was one of a long line of huge fortifications that a former Herod had built from the south to the north of the country. It was the most southerly, on the side of the Dead Sea across from the awe-inspiring sum- mer palace of Masada. Conditions in Machaerus must have been appalling. The summer heat in its dungeons would have beggared description. At this high point of Jesus' min- istry, word must somehow have got to John that a great movement was afoot. Luke makes it clear that John still had his own faithful following, ready to keep him posted about events and ready to help him in any way possible. This very fact is a measure of the man and his ability to keep friend- ships and loyalties through thick and thin.

We can only imagine his agony and frustration. Here was the fruit of all his labour coming to harvest, and he was to- tally isolated and helpless to take part. He was probably

29 August

quite aware that he was unlikely ever again to see the light of day. He decides to get a last message to Jesus. Somehow he succeeds, and the two messengers arrive at whatever place Jesus happens to be. The message is a blunt question, very much in John's unvarnished style: "Are you the one who is to come, or do we wait for another?"

We have no way of knowing whether Jesus had to consider for a while before replying. I suspect he did. Luke gives us the context of the moment. Jesus was surrounded by people. He had been engaged in a great deal of healing. Presumably he was both exhilarated by the response he was seeing and drained by the expectations and demands on him. We know from other such moments that Jesus sometimes had long thoughts about the reasons and motives for the following he was getting.

Suddenly he is faced with this uncompromising question from John. He knows well what kind of circumstances John is in. Jesus is fully aware of the desperation in the few short words, the anxiety with which his reply is awaited in the faraway, ghastly cell. He thinks for a few moments and then decides. "Go and tell John," he says, "what you have seen and heard." Then Jesus lists what is happening — blind people seeing again, the lame walking, lepers being healed, the deaf hearing again, the dead being raised, the poor hearing some good news. Every word of the reply is full of achievement, confidence, hope. The messengers thank him and turn away towards their journey back to the waiting prisoner.

There is something here that should give us pause, and also teach us about our situation today as Christians. We might consider for a moment another reply Jesus could have made, with equal evidence and equal validity. There was another side to the reality he was facing. He could have told those messengers to say to John that not everything was going well. There were many deaf people who did not wish to listen to him, many blind who were prepared to stay blind to what he wanted them to see, many in despair whose lives were lifeless and hopeless and who had no wish to come alive, many poor who were being treated with injustice and contempt, as they would be to the end of time.

If Jesus had sent that message back to John, he would have been relating a valid truth about the situation. But our Lord chose the evidence of hope. This is what we really need to see and to hear in our own contemporary moment of the gospel. We too seek to lead Christian lives in a very mixed context of life. The church seeks to be the church in that same mixed context. At any given time, and in reference to any given aspect of life, we may give the evidence of hope or the evidence of despair. The example of our Lord points to choosing the evidence of hope, if only for the fact that hope is essential to the enterprise of faithfulness. Our generation, as indeed any generation, is a captive in its own prison of time and history, as John was in his physical prison. Both John in his time and we in our time have doubts and fears. From our mutual prisons we ask the same question. We say to Jesus, We have believed in you, trusted you, given part of our lives to you. Are you the truth of God? We await his reply. It is most important to realize that his reply will always come to us in terms of hope, expectation, and encouragement, bidding us to dwell on the hopeful things in our situation.

Holy Cross Day

Almighty God,
whose Son our Saviour Jesus Christ
was lifted high upon the cross
that he might draw the whole world to himself,
may we who rejoice in the mystery of our redemption,
have grace to take up our cross and follow him,
who lives and reigns with you and the Holy Spirit,
one God, now and for ever.

Numbers 21.4b-9
Psalm 98.1-5
1 Corinthians 1.18-24   John 3.13-17

☙

If you can gain permission from the Orthodox Patriarch of Jerusalem, you will be guided down a wide stone staircase in the great Church of the Holy Sepulchre in the old city of Jerusalem. At the bottom of the stone steps is the cavernous Chapel of Saint Helena, and over to your left, a door in the wall. Step through this door, and you are in a different world. Gone are the smooth-cut stones of the building above you, the well-worn stairs, the icons, the altars, the hanging lights. Here you are in a world of naked light bulbs, iron ladders, and glistening, jagged quarry walls.

14 September

All around you the foundations of the great church, laid in the fourth century, go deep into the earth. Apart from your own movements and your own breathing or quiet speech, there is absolute silence. In that silence you can hear the voice of Macarius, Bishop of Jerusalem in the early fourth century, as he reads to himself the letter he has just received by imperial mail from his emperor.

> *The Victor Constantine, Maximus, Augustus.*
> *To Macarius.*
> You are an able man, and it is your task to make all the arrangements and plans for the construction of a basilica finer than any other. Moreover the rest of the buildings must also be made finer than those in any other city. *(It is a long letter)*
> Know that to our friend, the illustrious Dracilianus, Deputy of the Praetorian Prefects, and to the Governor of the Province, we have entrusted the planning and decoration of the walls. It is ordered, in my Piety, that they are to dispatch at once whatever in your judgment you may tell them is requisite in the way of craftsmen, laborers, and anything else for the building.
> When the plans have been drawn up, see that you write and inform us of the quantity of columns and marble you judge to be required to ensure that the building is as splendid as it should be. When we receive your estimate of the requirements, they can be supplied from all sources. The most wonderful place on earth deserves to be also the most splendid. I desire to know from you how the rood of the basilica is to be made. Is it to be coffered? If so, it may be gilded as well.
> God preserve you, dear brother. *(He ends with)*

I wonder where Macarius first read that letter? It is not impossible that he was standing where I am standing, although for him the surroundings would have been very different. Instead of being buried under the vast mass of a building, he would have been out under the sky, standing in the quarry whose jagged wall I can see by the light of this string of yellow bulbs. If the bishop were to climb to the edge of the quarry he would see the walls of the city a short distance to the east. This quarry was outside the city for a very good reason. (Macarius had only to turn to the north to look at the rough outcrop of stone that forms a small hill or knoll within the quarry;) on that hill the Romans crucified their condemned prisoners. I am sure that Macarius never looked at that crude rock outcrop without bowing his head or making some other gesture of respect, because he knew he was looking at the place where his Lord died in agony.

Macarius built as his emperor ordered him and he built well, so well that these walls, (though now changed in many ways from the original,) have withstood sixteen centuries of eventful and dangerous history. He and his workmen built a vast platform over the quarry, erected the walls of the basilica, and then crowned it with what was in those days the largest dome in the known world—so large, in fact, that when Omar came to Jerusalem in the seventh century at the head of the armies of Islam and decided to build the Dome of the Rock on the Temple site to the east, he unknowingly hired another generation of the same family of builders and ordered that his dome was to be slightly larger than that of the Church of the Holy Sepulchre. Tradition has it that the builders, being Christian, fudged their measurements, deceiving Omar and preserving the primacy of their earlier achievement.

We leave these dark, dimly lit foundations and climb again into the vast cavern of the basilica. Crossing the main rotunda we again face a flight of steps; this time we ascend them to a small, arched, shadowy chapel. Before us is an altar, and all around and behind it are the lamps familiar in every place of Orthodox worship. The air is warm because of the small candle burning in the hand of each person here. When my turn comes I crouch down as low as possible underneath the altar. There is a round hole in the floor, its edge surrounded by worn silver. Holding my small candle half behind me, I extend my right hand as far down as I can until it rests on cold, hard, rough stone. I let it rest there for a moment. A moment is all I can have because of the unending line of others who wait hour after hour, day in and day out, year after year, to do what I am doing.

I find myself silently saying a short personal prayer. It is less a prayer than a conviction of utter unworthiness beyond any words, but no less real and genuine for being inarticulate. I rise clumsily, but I don't care—it is not a place to preserve dignity or to draw attention to myself in any way. After all, I have touched the top of the small hillock that once stood under the sky in the quarry far below, whose walls I have seen half lost in the darkness of these foundations. My hand has touched the rock of Calvary where the cross once stood.

The place remains within me long after I leave it. One Sunday afternoon, when we knew we would be leaving Jerusalem in twenty-four hours to return home, my wife and I found that we both wished more than anything else to walk down to the Holy Sepulchre and sit in a corner of the chapel as the endless succession of visitors went by. We did this for about an hour, watching as individuals, couples, families with children—many of them local—came through. A father lifted two of his children to kiss the icon next to the altar, and now and then someone would have to be helped to position themselves under the altar. Often when they would rise they would be near to tears. It was quite late in the evening and the crowds had thinned out when we decided to leave. We lit two of the thin yellow tapers and placed them with whatever silent prayer each of us wished to offer; then we bent beneath the altar and once again touched the stone.

Mysteriously, it is not so much that you touch the stone as that you are touched by it; not so much that you encounter something as that you are encountered. Two Good Fridays have passed by since that experience and in each of those liturgies, beautiful and moving though they have been, I found that I now possess a reality greater than any words or music can convey.

I find myself thinking of the words with which John begins his letter: "We declare to you what was from the beginning, what we have heard, what we have seen with our eyes, what we have looked at and touched with our hands, concerning the word of life." As I think of these words, I give silent thanks that I have been able to touch with my hands the place where the cross of Jesus stood. I know that in itself this is not enough, that, as the collect says, I must have the grace to take up my cross and follow him. Yet having stood in the darkness of that ancient buried quarry and felt the coldness of the stone of Calvary, I find that the experience becomes grace to do so, and I am very grateful.

Saint Matthew

Almighty God,
who through your Son
called Matthew to be your apostle and evangelist,
free us from all greed and selfish love,
that we may follow in the steps of Jesus Christ our Lord,
who lives and reigns with you and the Holy Spirit,
one God, now and for ever.

Proverbs 3.1-6 or 2 Timothy 3.14-17
Psalm 119.33-40
Matthew 9.9-13

ℭℛ

I always think of Matthew when I walk down through the
gardens of the Church of the Beatitudes above the
north end of the lake of Galilee. Before you reach the
entrance you turn right—or left, for that matter—and move
on down through the gardens until you come out below the
building. You are at the top of the long green slope that goes
all the way down to the highway and the lakeshore just beyond. Far below you the lake stretches toward the south. It
is very likely that the sound of singing voices will be beginning just above you, one more of the almost endless masses
that are offered here hour after hour, day after day, by pil-

grims from every conceivable part of the world. That sound would be a joy to the ears of Matthew. He would know that his great bet had been won. His great courageous hunch that the new faith—new in his time—was headed for a long march into the future had been correct after all.

I have always imagined Matthew as a senior church bureaucrat. For me he is the consummate planner, a man good at details. I do not see him liking Mark's breathlessly hurried book or getting the least bit excited about Luke's vivid storytelling—if he ever got a chance to read them. Matthew is not above a good story himself, but he gives the impression that there is more important work to be done. The real purpose of his gospel is simple—not simple to do, but easy to express. It is the hammering together of an organization.

Matthew is the church organizer of the New Testament. If he lived among us in the late twentieth century, he would be writing endless books about church growth, parish programming, congregational development, stewardship, and adult education. Who would for one moment belittle his great gift to us? We need him today in our doubts and fears about what the church is and what it should be doing in today's world. Matthew would probably say to us that just as he and his contemporaries had to begin from scratch, so it is with us. It is becoming more and more obvious that the church that has carried us through to this point must once more change itself radically—or allow God to change it radically.

Matthew would point out to us that the church he and the others formed in those years after the crucifixion and the resurrection would not have recognized its medieval successor a thousand years later; in turn, that medieval church would not recognize itself in the church of the late twentieth century. If Matthew is the kind of person he appears to be in his gospel, I suspect that after a tour of today's church

136 ∽ HERALDS OF GOD

he would keep his criticisms to himself, simply suggesting that we face the fact that we must begin building the church again.

We owe Matthew a great deal. Above all we owe him his insight about those small scattered communities up and down his country. There they were in their small isolated groups, supporting one another to the degree they could, meeting to share the bread and wine, telling and retelling the stories they remembered about their Lord, all the time with one eye on the surrounding society in case it began to ask uncomfortable questions about the political acceptability of their gatherings. Nobody had as yet made the least attempt at what we would call today long-range planning. Life went on from day to day, from meeting to meeting.

Matthew's great insight was his realization that the skies were not going to split apart the day after tomorrow. It was not that he would ever have denied that his Lord would return—that was a given in his understanding of what had happened. But he was very aware that Mark had written his book with one eye on the sky, expecting the ascended Lord to appear at any moment and begin to wrap up the whole created order of things. It was becoming more and more obvious to more and more believers that the world had not ended, nor did it show any sign of doing so, and meanwhile a whole generation of believers was dying off. Some thoughtful people were beginning to suspect that Christian faith had to begin to think in terms of the long haul.

Matthew not only saw this, he also acted upon the insight. He sat down and began work on a book that was going to be the instrument to forge the organization that would be essential for the long march into the future. First he read Mark's gospel again and decided that, in spite of its apocalyptic assumptions, it was still a valuable instrument for the communities. Thus we learn something about Matthew we might otherwise miss, because he could so easily have dismissed Mark's work as naive and unrealistic, or sneered at its seemingly haphazard construction, or rejected it as totally unrelated to his own purpose. But he did not, and his not doing so is a lesson for our own time.

We have a tendency to dismiss the eagerness and the simplicity of evangelical faith as unrealistic and unsophisticated, setting itself up for disappointment by its unrelenting trust and optimism. Yet the guardedness and world-weariness that sometimes characterize conventional church life has to be challenged by such optimism and trust. Matthew saw that however long the church's future was to be, and however long Christians would have to hand on their faith from generation to generation, they would always need to balance their idea of a long future against the possibility that their Lord would make a sudden end of things, an end that would also be an unimaginably glorious new beginning. Matthew knew that he needed Mark, just as we know we will always need the vision of both evangelists.

Matthew would be very familiar with much of today's writing in the church. If he could read such books as *Resident Aliens* and *The Once and Future Church*, he would take note of their sense of massive dislocation, their realization that the position of the church in society had radically changed. Reading such books would have brought back to Matthew the immense sense of loss felt by his contemporaries at the destruction of the Temple in Jerusalem. It is quite likely that Matthew himself had often used the Temple to worship with other followers of the rabbi Jesus. It had provided a vast and ancient context for the community's life; now it lay in ruins. A new reality had to be faced, new questions had to be asked, new solutions found. What did it mean to be a follower of the Nazarene if all the symbolism and tradition of the Temple was gone, and you and your family were desperately trying to settle in to a huge cosmopolitan city like Antioch, where nobody cared in the least what you believed as long as you kept your nose clean with the local authorities? That sense of loss, of uprootedness, would have been well known to the men and women for whom Matthew sat down to write, just as they are well known today.

Matthew used his own Jewish background as a kind of scaffolding around which to design his book. Down in the town of Jamnia near the Mediterranean, the finest Jewish minds were coming to grips with what the new reality meant for them. With the Temple gone, what did it mean to be a Jew? They had made their decision: from then on, to be a Jew meant to trust in the five books of the Torah. That is why Matthew began to organize his own material in a pattern of five sections; when he began to think through how he was going to hand on his Lord's teaching, he forms it into five sections and sets us on that lovely hillside above the lake where Jesus preached the Sermon on the Mount. But behind and deep within those chapters, Matthew is telling us that for us Christians, Jesus is our Torah, our basis for trust and belief. Just as the Torah exists forever, so is Jesus forever Lord. If we have been given nothing else from this gospel—and we have been given immeasurably more—Matthew would have been quite satisfied with that.

Saint Michael & All Angels

Eternal God,
you have ordained and constituted in a wonderful order
the ministries of angels and mortals.
Grant that as your holy angels stand before you in heaven,
so at your command
they may help and defend us here on earth;
through Jesus Christ our Lord,
who lives and reigns with you and the Holy Spirit,
one God, now and for ever.

Genesis 28.10-17
Psalm 103.19-22
Revelation 12:7-12   John 1.47-51

℞

I n Brian Aldiss's science fiction thriller *Starship,* the
ship is a miniature world in which the crew and their
families have lived for so many generations that they no
longer know any other. For them the starship is the whole
world. From time to time the members of this community
glimpse larger beings, objects of fear and awe, who appear

from nowhere and then disappear again. Only at the end does Aldiss reveal a terrible truth about this crew and their families: for all these generations, they have never actually left the orbit of Earth. They are part of a millennia-long experiment in which they have become shorter, their body rhythms have changed, and their sense of time and season altered. The large, mysterious life forms they have glimpsed from time to time and about whom they tell stories and fables are human beings, technicians sent up from Earth to service the ship.

Why link this story with the feast of Saint Michael and All Angels? Because I suspect that it is a good description of the way most people think of angels, if they think about angels at all. The main difference between the appearances on our fictional ship and those of angels is that the angels' appearances are, we think, deliberate, and have a definite purpose. For example, Genesis tells of an encounter with angels very soon after we humans appear on the stage of creation, a meeting that is neither pleasant nor reassuring. When Adam and Eve are expelled from Paradise an angel is posted at the gate, flaming sword in hand, barring their return.

By the time we arrive at the last page of scripture we have had so many encounters with angels they have become like old friends. In the book of Revelation, John and his angel-escort saunter together by the river of life and take in the grandeur of the Holy City. The angel is quite alarmed when John falls down to worship him, insisting that he is no more than a fellow servant of God along with John himself and all the prophets.

Angels encounter us for an infinite number of reasons. They come in order to warn, to admonish, to guide, to rescue, to announce, to open prison doors, to sing anthems. They enter our lives at the most unexpected moments. Saint Luke wrote of a door opening in time and space in the hill village in Palestine where Gabriel appeared to Mary. The appearance to the young woman disturbs her because the angel enters not only into the outer world of time and space, but also into her inner world of awareness.

In heaven, too, we see contention and struggle as the great archangels gather their forces and war breaks out. Michael and Satan ride to battle and Michael triumphs, banishing Satan, hurtling him as a falling star from heaven to the depths of hell, and ever since Satan has won battle after battle among human beings because they are naive enough to think him defeated. They do not realize that he still possesses grandeur and power because he is an archangel, albeit a fallen one. We see this truth more clearly than anywhere else in Epstein's great bronze on the wall of Coventry Cathedral. Look quickly and you see Michael standing above a defeated Satan, apparently slain by his sword. Look again and you see that Michael's spear has not yet entered Satan's body, that Satan is not recumbent but propped on one elbow, about to rise. The struggle goes on forever and will not be resolved until the end of time.

In the same year that I write these lines the world of the dramatic arts has been confronted by one of the most powerful dramas of recent decades, Tony Kushner's *Angels in America*. This drama has put into words the dread and awe of the plague that has robbed every one of us of some friend or acquaintance, or has taken from us some greatly gifted man or woman whose art or humor or acting or writing or faith has graced our lives beyond measure. When Kushner set out to dramatize the terror and agony of AIDS, he found that it was impossible to do so without allowing human suffering a dimension beyond itself and beyond time and space. Only in that way could meaning be found for such suffering. With this choice he forced Western art to return to its ancient roots in Greek tragedy, where whatever happens on stage has a meaning beyond itself. There the voices of the chorus sang as the voice of the gods, or the gods themselves walked the higher reaches of the stage. All through the tradition of high opera the same devices are seen, where divine or satanic figures move in the world of human affairs. In the late twentieth century we suddenly find ourselves watching a stage where angels once again take their majestic place among us, bringing back dimension and depth to our living and dying, our loves and betrayals, our breaking hearts and vulnerable bodies.

Since angels come primarily to guide or to warn us, we need to ask ourselves about the times in our lives when we have been guided or protected—often from our worst selves. When we remember, then we need to recall the people we encountered at those times, realizing that in them we were encountering angels. Their wings and their glory were hidden, their voices were familiar and they spoke of everyday things. Yet when we remember such times and such people, we realize how much we have been guarded, protected, and guided, most often when we were completely unaware.

Two thousand years ago Joseph remembered when he awoke that an angel with great wings had warned him to take his wife and child to Egypt. His shoulder was shaken and his nostrils assailed by the midnight breath of some sleepy but courageous neighbor who had overheard a barroom conversation and decided to warn a stranger to get out of town before disaster struck. It is so easy to suppose that Elijah, sleeping the sleep of utter exhaustion as he fled from certain death by Jezebel's guards, remembered a flaming and majestic figure placing food before him in his periods of fitful wakefulness. But it may have been no more than the brief glimpse of a hand or a veiled face before it faded into the desert; such faces appear and fade soundlessly in the Sinai to this day.

29 September

Where both Joseph and Elijah differ from us, as they wake from their dreams and we wake from ours, is that they recognize these encounters as meetings with angels, angels who are ministers of grace. Our restless hearts will find no rest until, in the comings and goings of our daily lives, our ears are open to the beating of wings and our eyes can see the glory of Michael and his companions.

Saint Luke

Almighty God,
who inspired Luke the physician
to proclaim the love and healing power of your Son,
give your Church, by the grace of the Spirit
and the medicine of the gospel,
the same love and power to heal;
through Jesus Christ our Lord,
who lives and reigns with you and the Holy Spirit,
one God, now and for ever.

Sirach 38.1-4, 6-10, 12-14 or 2 Timothy 4.5-13
Psalm 147.1-7
Luke 4.14-21

☙

I have always imagined Saint Luke as about the age I am now—mature, graying perhaps, a little thin on top. I like my doctor to be the same age I am and I have always thought of Saint Luke as a doctor, ever since I first learned in school that the writer of this gospel was a physician. And I think he would have that quality the Romans used to call *gravitas*—it isn't quite the same as "grave" so perhaps we should translate it best as "seriousness," but the kind of seriousness that includes smiling. I imagine Luke with a white coat and stethoscope, even though I know he could not have had a stethoscope when he wrote the gospel, or with something that conveys the power and magic of a physician's place in our lives.

We met at a medical conference where I had been asked to give an address on some aspect of ethics. A number of people came up after the address to express appreciation, ask a question, offer an insight. He waited until the others had gone before introducing himself, looking almost exactly as I had expected, about my age, dressed quietly and tastefully. I got the impression of some sophistication, an easy self-confidence, a slight hint of amusement in the eyes. He suggested lunch.

"Of all the evangelists," I said to him after we had read through the menu and ordered, "you are the one I have wanted to meet the most."

"Why?" he inquired.

I hesitated, at a loss for an answer. It's always so much easier to say that one likes something or somebody than to say why. "Because when I put your two books beside the others," I said, "Mark seems like a tabloid—a little bit of this, a little bit of that, and Matthew is a bit too much like a bureaucrat with all his lists."

Luke looked as though he wanted to interrupt. I paused, to hear him say amusedly, "Surely you're not going to try to tell me that I did a better job than John!"

For a moment I was taken aback. "No, I'm not going to say that. I think what I want to say is that I still prefer your gospel to John's, even though comparing what you and John wrote is like comparing apples and oranges. We both know that what John did is magnificent, but what I like about you, now that you force me to define it, is your ability to tell a good story."

"I'm glad," he said, "That's what I wanted to do. Actually, that's what I had to do if I was going to get them to read it."

"Them?" I asked.

"The Romans, chiefly," he said. "Of course there were always others—you couldn't live and practice in a huge city like Antioch without coming across all kinds of people. But it was the Romans who really mattered in those days. Get their attention for something and you were all right. On the other hand, get them annoyed and you were in trouble."

"Is that why all your Roman characters come across as decent and attractive people?"

"In a way, yes. The fact is, many of them were. I've noticed how many people these days make stereotypes out of the characters in the gospels: all Pharisees are self-righteous, all Romans are cruel, all Greeks are wise—that sort of thing. Truth is, there were all kinds, even among the original community of followers. I should know! I tried to meet as many of them as I could."

"Of all of them, which one did you most enjoy meeting?"

Without the slightest hesitation he said, "The Lord's mother. It sounds a bit weak to say it, but she was a remarkable woman. I met her when she was fairly well on. Considering what she had been through, I assumed she would have aged beyond her years, and indeed she had aged, yet to be with her was to be in the presence of something you could never forget. She had a quality of life all her own, a luminous quality, as if she were full of light. You had the feeling it might blaze out at any moment and blind you."

"You were hearing and seeing her when you wrote those opening chapters?"

"Oh, yes," he said, and his eyes looked very far away. "Indeed I was. I still hear her and see her. I always will."

I felt I should move on. "Why did you write just when you did?" I asked.

"Because someone had to. Someone had to write down the story in a way that took it out beyond the narrowness of that world. You see, nobody, not even Mark and Matthew, saw that what had happened was as big as the world and all of time. That is what I had to get across." He leaned forward for emphasis. "By the time I got into the movement, Jerusalem was gone. The Romans had seen to that. Actually, to many of the believers it was this that made Rome enemy number one, and yet I could never accept that. Somehow I always knew that what had begun in Jerusalem had to move on to Rome as its next great stepping stone into the future."

"Is that why you wrote your second book?"

"It certainly was," he said, "and that is why I did a lot of things. That is why I made Jerusalem the stage for almost everything that happened after the Lord rose. I knew there had been other appearances—there were appearances all over the place and that was to be expected—but I just concentrated on Jerusalem. That is why I ended the second book when I got Paul to Rome."

"Did you intend a third?"

He smiled. "Ask anyone who writes a book! If you write one you always think about another. After that, it never lets you alone. The answer to your question is yes, but there was not enough time."

I wanted to ask what exactly he meant. Did he mean lack of hours in the day, or did something happen?

"I have to go soon," said Luke. "I didn't think I would be interested in the sessions at this conference, but I find them fascinating. One thing that intrigues me is the way things haven't changed, such as the doctor-patient relationship. But before I go, let me tell you quickly a couple of other reasons why I wrote those two books. Actually, I wrote them as one book because, as I told you already, I saw with utter clarity that the Lord was for all time and for all humanity. As the first few years went by in Antioch and reports came in from Paul and Barnabas, it became more and more obvious that nationality, race, language, culture—none of these were barriers to the Lord. I decided to close my practice and travel with Paul for a while to see for myself, and I did indeed see wonderful things happening. Speaking of Paul, he was a big reason for my writing about the events after the Lord had risen—absolutely the right man at the right time. I am quite certain God had put a hand on him directly.

"My last reason for writing was that I saw something missing from both Mark and Matthew. They seemed to have missed the quality in the Lord that for me shone out above everything else, and that was his infinite capacity for welcoming people into his life. But it wasn't just that. It was the sheer numbers of people he welcomed. Nobody was outside his acceptance, no matter how poor or insignificant. Have you any idea how many people were dismissed in those days as irrelevant, as if their lives were of no significance whatsoever? You must have, because I can see you people have the equivalent today. For us it was women, children, Samaritans, invalids, lepers, tax people…the list goes on, as I'm sure yours does. For the Lord, every one of these was within the circle of acceptance—more than acceptance, the circle of love."

"You don't mean that you literally saw him," I said, making it sound less like a statement than a question.

He smiled. "Of course I saw him, countless times. I saw him in eyes and voices and faces all around me. I saw him at tables where we shared bread and wine. Did I see him in a literal sense? No. But it's that literalism of yours that makes you go into such agonies trying to analyze what I and the others wrote. Anyway, that's another story. I must go."

I reached for the bill. He looked back and said, "I charged it to my room. We doctors always feel we should pay the bill. After all, even back in my time we did pretty well." He laughed, turned away, and was lost in the lines of people heading for the afternoon sessions.

Saint Simon &
Saint Jude

Almighty God,
we thank you for the glorious company of the apostles,
and especially on this day for Simon and Jude.
As they were faithful and zealous in their mission,
so may we with ardent devotion
make known the love and mercy
of our Lord and Saviour Jesus Christ,
who lives and reigns with you and the Holy Spirit,
one God, now and for ever.

Deuteronomy 32.1-4 or Ephesians 2.13-22
Psalm 119.89-96
John 15.17-27

ଔ

W hy is it so difficult to get rid of the suspicion that
both of these men are afterthoughts? Simon and
Jude are always at the tail end of the list of the
disciples, and even their day is almost at the end of the holy

days, right up against All Saints. The book linked with Jude's name is the last book in the New Testament before Revelation. It might have only taken one further nudge for both Simon and Jude to have been consigned to oblivion in Christian memory, but here they are, complete with a feast day, a collect, and three readings, not to mention a psalm, all held to these two by the most tenuous of links!

The collect works hard at forging some links. The clues lie in the words "zealous" and "ardent devotion"—impressive words to put the best light possible on an ugly reality. To trace that reality we need to go on a journey.

We are driving along the northern shore of the lake, heading east. These are the miles where one is conscious of being on the central stage of the gospels. Tiberias is behind us on the highway, as is Magdala; ahead and far above us is the Convent and Church of the Beatitudes. Soon, immediately to our right, we will see Tabgha, where the multiplication of the loaves and fishes is memorialized by the Benedictines in what is probably the most authentic re-creation possible of a fourth-century church. Just beyond it stands the Franciscan shrine of Mensa Domini with its delicate and graceful bronze of the risen Lord calling Peter on the shore. A few minutes later we will pass Capernaum, its walled ruins a mecca for thousands daily. Unseen in the slopes to the left are the buried remains of Chorozin, mentioned in passing by Jesus. From there, we pass where Bethsaida once stood.

It is just possible that this area was home to Simon, since this part of the province was noted for its revolutionaries in our Lord's day. Not that they could live here in peace and quiet; as soon as they became involved in terrorist activities they would have had to head for the higher and more remote parts of the province to the north and to the east. But those areas are not far away, and we are about to explore one of them.

On we go, the gears of the bus grinding a little from time to time, passengers swaying in the sharp ungraded curves. We are beginning to climb into the Golan. As soon as we reach the top we head northeast across the plateau, every so often spotting signs of army activity. Eventually we turn off the highway and drive slowly into the grounds of a national park. We are at Gamla—or near it. To reach it is another story; it is not for nothing that this place is sometimes called the Masada of the north.

We move through the entrance of the park and head across the fields until we are standing at the edge of an escarpment. We are looking at something wild and grand, a deep, precipitous valley winding away to the north. It is two valleys, really, parallel to one another and divided by a high, steeply sloped backbone of rock. This is the physical feature that gives this place its name; Gamla means simply "camel." We are looking at a giant camel's hump carved by nature. A closer look shows ruins extending down the west side of the hill. It is easy to imagine what the town once looked like, not unlike a Greek village tiered down the slopes of an Aegean island. That likeness quickly ceases when we realize what this town was built for and what happened here.

Gamla became a fortress town for the Zealot movement around the time that Simon was a child down by the lake and Jesus a small boy back over the hills in Nazareth. Here the Zealots thumbed their noses at the Romans, secure in the knowledge that Gamla was impregnable; not for the first or last time did they miscalculate Roman determination and ingenuity. The siege of Gamla is one of history's most shocking tragedies, less well known than you might expect only because of even worse horrors in the decades to follow. In its last hours hundreds of Jewish families hurled their children from the sheer cliffs at the end of the gigantic outcrop on which they had built their town, and then leaped to their own deaths rather than face Roman retribution.

It is almost certain that the adult Simon would at some time in his life have come here and stood where we stand. For him the memory of Gamla, still fresh in his parents' memory, would have been sacred and infinitely romantic, as was the Zealot movement he had joined. One of the most intriguing questions of the New Testament is how and why a man like Simon, committed to the most savage and unrelenting struggle for national rights, became involved with the gentle rabbi from Nazareth, with his dream of a sacred kingdom of justice and peace. All we know is that he is there in the group, there in the upper room, and there in the gathering in Jerusalem following the mysterious parting we call the ascension.

No matter how little we know of Simon, we know even less of Jude. All we know is that the fierce, short diatribe called the book of Jude is, ironically, an exercise in verbal zealotry! Is this why Simon and Jude became teamed up in Christian memory, one a warrior of the sword, the other of the pen? A quick reading of Jude leaves one almost breathless with its ferocity against those who harbored undesirable theologies in that community of long ago. A brief list of words gives the general tenor: "contending for the faith...destroyed those who did not believe...kept in eternal chains...punishment of eternal fire...contended with the devil...destroyed." This list is then followed by a wild outbreak of name calling directed at these unknown deviants from the true path:

They are blemishes on your love-feasts....They are waterless clouds carried along by the winds; autumn trees without fruit, twice dead, uprooted; wild waves of the sea;...wandering stars, for whom the deepest darkness has been reserved forever.

As with many New Testament books, we can only speculate about the actual author, because we may be dealing with an unknown author anchoring his claim for significance to some earlier apostolic figure. In either case, we end up in the company of the person we know in the apostolic band as Jude or, as he is carefully designated, "Judas, not Iscariot."

It is a sad way to have your name remembered through the centuries, set off by nothing more than a careful disassociation from a better-known villain. Yet this is the only way we have of defining Jude. Like Simon, he is always at the tail end of the apostolic list without a single line to say in the drama. Because of his association with Simon the Zealot, coupled with the fierceness of the short book that bears his name, it is not impossible that he too was a member of the Zealot movement.

If he was, we have to ask the same question that haunts us about Simon: what was it that brought Jude into the company of Jesus of Nazareth? Jesus' dream was far from the blood-soaked revolution of the Zealots. His hand held no spear to kill and wound, but the power to heal. He had no vision of the Romans banished from his land; Jesus' dealings with them were, if anything, friendly. In the eyes of men like Simon and Jude he could well have been dismissed as a collaborator. Yet in spite of all these differences these two come to form the circle of his disciples. It is useless to wonder why—it is enough to acknowledge that he changed them as he changed so many others who encountered him.

Throughout history Christians have tended to weave endless tales of extravagant achievement around the lives of apostles they know almost nothing about. In the case of Simon and Jude, we hear of them doing deeds of daring in faraway Persia, where they meet a suitably horrendous and dramatic martyrdom. Is this because we have drawn back from acknowledging that they may have gone on to live ordinary and uneventful lives? Why can't we imagine them returning to the lakeside with their memories of the events that changed everything for them, responding from time to time to some request from leaders like Peter and Paul and James, but for the most part building an intimate community in the little world they knew and that had formed them? What is wrong with this possibility? After all, millions of us who are called to faith by the same Lord live out our allegiance in ordinary and uneventful lives, yet we do not take each other less seriously for it.

The collect for this day offers some good advice on this topic. It points out that we give thanks not so much for individuals, great or obscure as they may be, but for "the glorious company of the apostles." We are saying thank you for a *community* rather than for individuals—a very useful corrective to our tendency to think of gifts as primarily individual rather than communal. It reminds us that our Lord's great statement about the location of the kingdom of heaven tells us that it is *among* us.

All Saints

Almighty God,
whose people are knit together in one holy Church,
the mystical Body of your Son,
grant us grace to follow your blessed saints
in lives of faith and commitment,
and to know the inexpressible joys you have prepared
for those who love you;
through your Son Jesus Christ our Lord,
who lives and reigns with you and the holy Spirit,
one God, now and for ever.

A	*Revelation 7.9-17*	*Psalm 34.1-10*
	1 John 3.1-3	*Matthew 5.1-12*
B	*Revelation 21.1-6a*	*Psalm 24.1-6*
	Colossians 1.9-14	*John 11.32-44*
C	*Daniel 7.1-3, 15-18*	*Psalm 149*
	Ephesians 1.11-23	*Luke 6.20-36*

℞

The first light of dawn touches one of the most barren mountain ranges in the world, deep in the south Sinai. For the last few hours a small group of pilgrims has climbed the winding path that leads to the summit of Mount Sinai. Far below, hidden in the great ocean of barren rock that forms this part of the world, is the fortress monastery of Saint Catherine, its community dating from the fourth century, its vast buildings from the sixth. Quite apart from this mountain, the monastery itself is an image of the long line of succeeding Christian generations we think of at this season.

On the summit this group of travelers—all Anglican—are joined by a group of Korean Pentecostal Christians, as well as a group of Orthodox. All want to mark this moment in some special way: the Koreans shout their gospel choruses, the Anglicans read from Exodus about the giving of the Law and then sing a hymn, and the Orthodox chant some beautiful and haunting passage from their liturgy. As the pilgrims return down the mountain, they realize that they all have been given a glimpse of the meaning of the feast of All Saints.

Part of that meaning is remembering the generations of men and women before us who have in innumerable ways served our Lord. We also need to recognize that millions who live among us and around us in our own lifetime are also faithful in countless ways, and therefore we can look to a future that holds out the possibility of an innumerable host of people who will in their own way and time serve the same Lord. We need to let the wonder of this reverberate in our minds, and to let its significance lift our hearts and enlarge our frequently troubled and anxious souls.

All Saints and its images can come to us as a blessing in this time when we struggle with some harsh realities facing Christian faith and the Christian churches. We can sum these up in the question, "How will Christian faith be expressed and what will be the structures of Christian community in the millennium ahead?" As we ask this question in endless books, articles, conferences, and speeches, as we seek to work toward answers in endless programs, planning strategies, and experiments, we need to be aware of the call that comes to us each year when this season returns. The feast of All Saints asks us to keep before our eyes the vast reality and infinite variety of the Christian community, and to place all our questions, fears, and anxieties in that larger context. This is exactly what John of Patmos does for the early Christians at a time when they too had many questions, fears, and anxieties about the future. Small wonder that we choose him as one of the voices to speak to us at this time of the Christian year.

To remember the past is always in some measure to encounter ourselves, with our difficulties and our questions, in other people at other times. Realizing this is crucial to our morale. On the other hand, anticipation gives hope. If I am offered a vision of countless other people as yet unborn who will eat the sacred bread that I eat, drink the sacred wine that I drink, and name the same Jesus Christ that is on my lips, then I possess hope. I no longer have to see myself as the last rank of a bedraggled army stumbling to this point in history, which is precisely the image of the church in the minds of many of its people.

As the twentieth century draws to a close, the yearly celebration of All Saints' Day is teaching something that we in the Western world are not finding easy to learn. Slowly and reluctantly we are being forced to realize that the West is only one small corner of Christian witness. All too easily we equate the West with Christian faith; even if we are aware of Christians in almost every part of the globe, we tend to see them as subordinate to us and very often dependent on us. With every passing year we are coming to see that not only is this untrue, it was never true!

What of the saints themselves? When we hear the word "saint," what comes to mind? For a long time there was a tendency to think of a saint as larger than life, because it is very difficult to study the tradition and not to conclude that saints are spiritual giants. It is hard to put out of your mind the stained-glass windows, the Renaissance carvings and sculpture, the bronze figures of Saint Michael and Satan on the wall of Coventry Cathedral, the great cosmic circles of Orthodox mosaics with their stern, dark-eyed faces emanating wisdom, strength, and authority. Our visions of sainthood tend to be highly romantic. There has been a long tradition of hermit saints of the desert, but we in the West have never really taken them to our hearts because of their austerity and their strangeness, their psychological oddities. Ironically, the same is true of these men and women who embody the spirituality of Celtic Christianity, but for some reason these seem to be enjoying great esteem and popularity! I am sure all of them must be laughing in heaven.

On the whole, however, we have become more realistic about saints. For one thing, we are more open to the possibility of encountering sainthood around us in everyday life. Congregational life is often aware of a few quiet saints whose very presence enriches and graces the worshiping community.

For me, the most insightful remark about sainthood comes from the science-fiction writer Ursula LeGuin in her book *Dancing at the Edge of the World,* even though she was not speaking of sainthood in religious terms. She imagines that a spaceship comes along and offers room for one passenger, one exemplary human being from whom a faraway race can learn what human beings are all about. To find this person, LeGuin says, she would go down to the marketplace and pick an old woman over sixty who

> has worked hard at unimportant jobs all her life, jobs like cooking, cleaning, bringing up kids, selling little objects of adornment to other people. She was a virgin once, then a

sexually potent female, and then went through menopause. She has given birth several times and faced death several times—the same times. Every day now she is facing the final birth/death a little more nearly. Sometimes her feet hurt. She never was educated to anything like her capacity, and that is a waste and a crime. She has a stock of sense, wit, patience, and experiential shrewdness.

LeGuin goes on to say that only someone who has experienced and accepted the entire human condition—the most essential quality of which is change—can represent human being. She is not speaking overtly of Christian sainthood, but I suspect that if we were looking for the quintessential saint, we could do worse than to follow her advice.

All Souls

Father of all,
we pray to you for those we love, but see no longer.
Grant them your peace,
let light perpetual shine upon them,
and in your loving wisdom and almighty power,
work in them the good purpose of your perfect will;
through Jesus Christ our Lord,
who lives and reigns with you and the Holy Spirit,
one God, now and for ever.

Wisdom 3:1-9   Psalm 116.1-8
1 Peter 1:3-9
John 6:37-40 or John 11:21-27

‎☙

When I was a child in the south of Ireland, there was no great effort made to shield children from the reality of death, for the simple reason that it was not possible to do so. To a far greater degree than today, everyone lived out almost all their lives in their own neighbourhood, and shared within it every aspect of life. Very little could be hidden. We children played on the street — every house familiar, every face easily named. Sickness was immediately known, to be spoken of in whispers. Deformities were much more frequently seen, as were bodily afflictions such as goitres, skin lesions, and tumours. The elderly almost invariably lived and died at home, if only because the resources of medicine were very limited; and therapies, beyond sympathy and loving care, were as yet unknown.

In our world death assumed a certain majesty. It would become known that someone was dying. We children would note the house, instinctively distancing ourselves, careful that a ball was not kicked against its walls or into its small garden. Eventually other signs of death's coming would appear. A neighbour would enter, stay a while, and emerge weeping. A motor car might come — unusual on the street — indicating the arrival of the doctor, always formally dressed and complete with a small leather bag. Some time later a priest would arrive, perhaps in street clericals or in cassock and biretta. His coming was the certain indication that the shadow was falling across our little world. Later the yellow blinds would be lowered on the windows, and a length of black crepe would hang from the knocker on the door. The final and most fascinating moment for us children would be the arrival of the coffin, its polished wood and brass handles shining in the late afternoon sun as it disappeared into the house. Our fevered imagination would conjure up what must be happening behind the silent facade of the house, until the coffin emerged, to be carried into the waiting hearse, followed by the family and those neighbours who had gathered outside. The glass doors would open to receive the coffin. The driver and his assistant, resplendent in black top hats, would climb aloft. The great black horses would respond to the reins, and the slow cavalcade would move off towards the chapel, slowly disappearing around the end of the street. We children would stand for a moment in awed silence until the spell would break, the ball would be kicked back into play, and death would be banished in our frenzied shouting, pushing, and running.

Future historians will be intrigued that in the late twentieth century death became unfashionable. Just as in the previous century sex was banished from polite conversation, so in the twentieth, death suffered the same fate. However, since death, like sex, is something of an enduring reality, it cannot be so easily willed out of existence by the fiat of fashion, and has become known by many other names. Today very few people die. They are "lost." Someone may say, "I am sorry to hear that you lost your spouse." People also "pass away" or "are no longer with us" or, yet again, "have been taken from us."

If in our time the term *death* has become unfashionable, so also has the word *soul*. There was a time when everyone had a soul. It was impossible to conceive of a living human being as not having a soul. He or she might well be a monster of evil, but it was still assumed that within the person there was a soul. Then, as with death, the soul ceased to be fashionable. Again, as with death and sex, the tendency to deny the existence of the soul was inconvenienced by the fact that people are obviously much more than warm bodies. They are even more than minds. What then do we call this "more"? To fill this need we have turned to words given to us by various psychologies. We decided many years ago that it was acceptable to use the term *super ego*, a particularly attractive term that gave us the opportunity to display some knowledge of Freud, who was European and therefore, intriguingly, slightly wicked. More recently we gave ourselves permission to use the terms *anima* or *animus*, terms given us by an equally attractive mentor, Carl Jung.

For those who chose not to use these terms, or who did not know them, there was the useful word *spirit*. Unfortunately this word has also been found invaluable in the world of advertising to express particularly vague and meaningless entities, such as the ability of an automobile to capture "the spirit of the highway," or the ability of some garment or some hair shampoo to impart "a spirited look."

But suddenly the soul is back with us. To use the word soul in a book is no longer to risk public rejection. We see best sellers on the subject of the soul. This return of the soul to cultural acceptance is part of something greater — the release of the Western mind from the prison we have constructed over the last three centuries, in the name of our being enlightened. The return of the concept of the soul also means that we are being released from the prison of mere time and being given back the gift of eternity. For whatever else the mysterious reality we call the soul means, it refers to that part of our humanity that is not the prisoner of time. With us and in us the soul does indeed live in time, and is affected only too obviously by that experience, but it cannot be held by time. In its experience of time the soul may become a great soul, a miserable soul, a noble soul, or an evil soul; but this does not change its being an eternal soul.

The moment we say such things of the soul, we begin to see why our century has found so many ways to avoid the word and what it has always meant. If we are indeed souls destined for eternity, then in this present life we are certainly accountable for what we say and do, and for who we are, a possibility not happily heard by a society of super egos, ids, *animas*, and shadows. To use such terms is not to dismiss the very real truths they express for us. Each expresses a very valid element in our make-up, but none has ever claimed the ultimacy we mean when we speak of the soul. My personal conviction is that soul, by its very nature, is beyond definition.

There may be more than one reason why the season we call All Souls came into the life of the church. The tapestry of Christian time is many layered, but one reason seems cer-

5

tain. The feast of All Saints celebrated those great lives in which words and deeds seemed in their various ways to have made a difference. During the Middle Ages, with the awareness and concern about death, there began to be further concerns about the untold hosts of people who were born, lived out seemingly ordinary lives, and died. What of them? What did such lives mean, short and harsh as was the fate of many of them. What was the Christian hope for this vast multitude?

To respond pastorally the church spoke, as it still speaks in this collect, of "those we love, but see no longer." Again, in the words of the Wisdom tradition, which is full of the unflinching realism of Judaism, the misery and abandonment felt in the face of death is fully acknowledged, while at the same time we are assured that "the souls of the righteous are in the hand of God and no torment will ever touch them." The words have something of the simplicity and unconditional assurance we offer a child. "Where is Mummy?" a small voice asks before the instinctive terror of the unknown. Arms tighten around the child and a voice replies, "Mummy is with God in heaven." There is probably no other reply that can be wiser or more true at such a moment. The chosen words of the gospel suggest such a reply, hinting that, as Lazarus is called back into being, so we, having said our farewells at life's ending, find ourselves called into new being by one who names us and says, "Come forth."

Such is the song of All Souls, a song of hope. I can recall how in the innocence of childhood we watched the coffin emerge from the small house, knowing that someone utterly familiar would never again watch us at play, yet in the same moment taking it for granted that their soul was, if not already in heaven, at least in purgatory and being prepared for heaven. Was this merely the simple faith of childhood, or is it the most sublime hope ever offered to souls born to live and to die, yet longing always for eternity?

Saint Andrew

Almighty God,
who gave your apostle Andrew
grace to believe in his heart
and to confess with his lips that Jesus is Lord,
touch our lips and our hearts
that faith may burn within us,
and we may share in the witness of your Church
to the whole human family;
through Jesus Christ our Lord,
who lives and reigns with you and the Holy Spirit,
one God, now and for ever.

Deuteronomy 30.11-14 or Romans 10.8b-18
Psalm 19.1-6
Matthew 4.18-22

☙

T he tree is a little uncomfortable, pressing against the small of my back, but all in all the stay here on the lakeshore is pleasant. We are on the east side of the lake, which tends to be quieter than the west side. One good reason for the quiet is that we are immediately under the ridge called the Golan; there was a time when to be here at all was dangerous. These days a couple of army patrols share this part of the shoreline, doing what we are doing—enjoying lunch.

There are no towns around here and no shops for quite a ways up and down the road, so if you forget your lunch there is nowhere to get any. Realizing this is just a short step from thinking of the problem they had somewhere around here a long time ago—and not just one person without lunch but, if their numbers are correct, a formidable five thousand. As I eat my sandwich of processed ham, unripe tomato, and limp cucumber, I find myself thinking about Andrew. Today the lake is choppy on an early spring day, still cold enough for a down jacket, and I wonder idly what kind of day it was that he stood somewhere around here desperately trying to think of something to save the situation. I continue to eat, wondering what he looked like, how he sounded, how he acted under pressure. I get the strong impression that he was a good man to have around when things got a little uncomfortable.

My clue to Andrew lies in that word "readily" in the second line of his collect: Andrew had such grace, we are told, that he *readily* obeyed Jesus' call. Grace is an elusive and mysterious word. In this case is the grace in that he *readily* obeyed, rather than grudgingly, carefully, tentatively? Is there a suggestion that to do anything willingly, readily, and cheerfully has a kind of grace about it? People like I imagine Andrew to be seem to radiate an openness to life, a vitality, a celebration of the very fact that we are alive and can respond to life and the God of life with all our being. Henri Nouwen calls such graciousness an attitude of hospitality. Perhaps Andrew's finest achievement was his ability to bring people into our Lord's presence. He possessed the grace to get others to risk approaching the source of all grace.

Maybe it would help us understand Andrew's grace better if we went back and discovered exactly what Andrew did and said. Saint John remembered these things in detail when he wrote his gospel years later. Who knows, perhaps Peter told him—or perhaps Andrew did himself.

Andrew first met Jesus at an embarrassing and sensitive moment. He had been looking for a focus in his life for some time and he thought he had found it in the electrifying energy and passion of John the baptizer, but John's movement did not seem to be going anywhere at that stage. John, too, knew that he had gone as far as he could go. The torch was passing.

One day when Andrew and a friend were talking to John, Jesus happened to be nearby. They follow after him, their sense of quest written so obviously all over them that Jesus has merely to turn and say, "What are you looking for?" Jesus plays them like a consummate fisherman. When they ask him, "Where are you staying?" it is obvious they are ready to talk the rest of the day through. The welcome they receive is warm and relaxed and casual. "Come and see," says Jesus.

The day after this encounter, Andrew is already eager to start in whatever direction Jesus points. If the Bible indulged more readily in exclamation marks, there would surely be one after his excited shout to his brother Peter: "We have found the Messiah!" Notice what Andrew does *not* say. He does not say, "I think there is someone you should meet. Perhaps you and I can chat afterward and you can tell me what you think." None of these niceties for Andrew—he is in up to the neck, eager to involve anyone, even his brother Peter, who, if the truth were known, has probably often told him to simmer down and stop babbling.

And it works. Peter comes. Is there just the slightest hint that he comes grudgingly and warily? Was it partly Peter's expression that made our Lord later refer to a certain stony attitude when they first met? But, stony or not, Peter comes, drawn by the infectious enthusiasm of Andrew.

If Andrew did not have this quality before he met our Lord, he seems to have picked it up naturally as he turned into the great go-between of the gospel adventure. He had the capacity to make links between people without threatening them or alienating them in any way. Andrew attracted people to each other by first attracting them to himself—not for his own sake, but to pass them on to our Lord. Three times it happened. It seems to be the one thing John the Evangelist wanted us to recognize and remember about Andrew.

We see Andrew's magic twice more. The next time is about a year after this first encounter with Jesus, on a hillside, with a hungry crowd that numbers in the thousands. Nobody knows what to do with all these people, but Andrew goes off and returns with a boy who is probably not at all sure about handing over his small meal of loaves and fishes. If on this particular occasion Judas, the most practical of men, had taken one look and muttered something about Andrew's typical impracticality, Andrew would not have cared. He is already aware that what he has brought may be useless—John's gospel recalls that Andrew even said so. But Andrew has done what he can do best; he has exercised his gift in making the link between Jesus and the boy, and he knows there is someone with a greater gift to take over from there.

Some people are just natural go-betweens. They make it possible for deals to be made between unlikely partners and they know how to effect the most difficult introductions. They have the ability to find exactly the right moment to step forward without intruding. This is what happened the second time we see Andrew's magic. Not knowing that Andrew is the man they need, a group of Greeks who have heard about Jesus ask Philip if they might speak to the teacher. Philip knows exactly where to turn—to Andrew, who gracefully makes the introduction. One suspects he is almost invisible as he does so, that never for one moment does he get in the way of whatever conversation ensues.

Perhaps Andrew's grace lives in this ability to be a go-between; it is the grace of self-effacement for the sake of others. Perhaps it may not seem the most dazzling aspect of grace, but without it the world would be a good deal poorer.

It is interesting that Matthew's gospel tells the story of Andrew's call in a different way. He says that the two brothers were mending their nets when Jesus appeared. Who knows? There is no reason why they could not have been chatting to John the baptizer at the same time. What is important for our knowledge of Andrew is that Matthew tells us that they followed Jesus *immediately*. We say of someone we have loved for many years, "When we met I immediately knew this was the person for me." The days when love was being sown, the weeks and months when love was growing, deepening, and blossoming have gone from memory. There remains only the immediacy of love. Andrew would have understood this.

*Appendix**

Saint James of Jerusalem

Grant, O God, that following the example of your servant James the Just, brother of our Lord, your Church may give itself continually to prayer and to the reconciliation of all who are at variance and enmity; through Jesus Christ our Lord, who lives and reigns with you and the Holy Spirit, one God, now and for ever.

Acts 15:12-22a 1 Corinthians 15:1-11
Matthew 13:54-58

ᙅᙠ

H e was there before even the earliest disciple. He probably knew the narrow alleys of Nazareth like the back of his hand. In later years he could remember all the little things of family life, the times his brother got into trouble, the wrestling matches they had, the freezing winter days when they had to share duty on the

---

* This selection is for a Holy Day in the Episcopal Church, and appears in sequence in the U.S.A. edition of this book.

---

surrounding hills to look after the family goats and sheep
because Joseph their father had given orders and that was
that. He remembered their petty likes and dislikes, all the
things that used to annoy their mother, all the things that
make family life what it is: a mixture of joys and frustra-
tions, hurts and healing.

His name was James and he was one of four. His parents'
names were Mary and Joseph, and he grew up in a hill village in Galilee. When he was in his late twenties his whole
family got involved with the Jerusalem police because of his
brother; then, to top it all off, he discovered many people
were beginning to believe that his dead brother was God. At
first he decided that it was their business and not his. Then
something happened to make it his.

When I met James I was standing about fifty yards to the
east of the Al Aqsa mosque looking out over the battle-
mented walls of the Temple Mount toward the top of the
Mount of Olives. It is at this point that the vast construction of Herod is at its highest point above the Kidron valley.
More than a hundred and twenty feet below, the ground
slopes steeply away to the even more distant bottom of the
valley.

It was not until he spoke that I became aware of the
heavy-set figure beside me. "It's a long way down, isn't it,"
he observed quietly.

"Yes," I replied. "Herod didn't do things by halves."

"It was one of the Herods who ordered that I be thrown
from there," he said, pointing with his stick at the corner of
the battlements. "Even after that fall I was still conscious—in agony, but conscious. I would have been left
there as long as it took for me to die, but a friend risked
coming and ending it quickly for me."

He extended a hand. "My name is James. I'm the one who had the job of holding things together in Jerusalem in the very early days."

"You're his brother," I said.

"Yes," he replied, "but to introduce myself that way makes it complicated. One of the things about being his brother is that I have a thousand memories, just as you have of your own brothers."

"Was there any particular reason why you never wrote anything down about all those years?"

"Well, that's a question we wouldn't have asked," he said. "Biography as you know it was not really part of our lives or our culture. Anyway, those years were pretty ordinary; we played and argued and fought. Why would you want a book about that? Later on, when we were adolescents, something changed. He was quieter and he would go off alone, but most people go through that, growing up. He never took himself out of the family in any obvious way. He was always ready to be part of the chores, part of the changing responsibilities, especially after our father died. Now that I think back, if there was any difference between him and the rest of us it was in the way he related our to mother. Their relationship was more complex and subtle than his relationship with the rest of us, and because he was the oldest we naturally did what he said. He could be tough sometimes, but he was always fair.

"Where we really disagreed was when he embarked on the public chapter of his life. By that time the family had split up and the rest of us were married, though we all lived in the same area. His going around in public was hard on all of us. We tended to get either the stares of those who worshiped the ground he walked on or the sneers of those who thought he was public enemy number one. That wasn't easy, believe me!"

"What about that time in Nazareth when the authorities sought your help in reining him in a little?" I asked.

"The crowds he attracted were getting larger and larger, so that various people were beginning to come up from Jerusalem to check up on him from the Temple security agencies. Everyone was very edgy and several people actually came to us in Nazareth to tell us he was drawing crowds down by the lake in Capernaum. They asked Mother if she could use her influence to get him to tone things down for a while.

"Well, you know what happened once we got there. When he was told we were outside on the edge of the crowd, he just told everyone it didn't matter, that anyone who followed him was his mother and brother. If there was a particular moment when I withdrew from him, it was then—I was furious at him."

"Then what brought you into the movement afterward?" I asked.

For a moment he was quiet; he seemed to be framing some kind of reply. "He came to me," he said simply.

"Came to you?"

"Yes. After he"—James hesitated—"died. You remember the list Paul made, the list of the times my brother came—well, appeared—to people? Paul included me in the list, and it was true. I never hid it. I couldn't. It changed everything for me."

James leaned back from me a little as if he needed some breathing space. "Can you imagine what it meant for me to acknowledge"—again the hesitation—"the truth? To acknowledge what had been the reality all those years of growing up, and to remember certain moments, certain things said and done together, all a completely different way? Can you imagine?"

"You really did get involved," I said. "You took on the responsibility for all the activities in the Jerusalem area, all the arguments and the stresses in the various factions."

"I did," said James with a weary laugh, "and God knows I had to exercise every talent I had for reconciling people. That's really what I became known for, walking a tightrope between yelling groups, trying to get a reasonable compromise. That was what I did all the time. Not that it stops people from getting angry at you for not coming down on their side. But that's the way life is." He shrugged.

"I said yes to taking on major responsibility in the movement because I could see clearly that was what he wished to bring about. He didn't do what he did just to become the focus of a vague spirituality, whatever that is. He did what he did to bring into being a community here and now that would somehow"—he groped again for words—"that would somehow reflect a vision of the kind of community we can't have here in time and history, the kind of community he meant when he spoke of what he called the kingdom of God."

"We're having real difficulties with that ourselves," I said. "We're experiencing so much stress in the community right now."

"I know that," said James, "and I wish it could be easier for you. I can't wave a magic wand for you, but there is one thing I would warn you against. Don't go around with the idea that this is something new, because there has never been a time when the community hasn't been under enormous stress. The simple truth is that the gulf between the actual church and the vision we have of it will always be enormous. My God, when you come to think of it, if it wasn't that enormous he wouldn't have had to go through what he did to make it possible."

He paused, realizing we had been chatting quite a while and the area was filling up with tourists. "Time to go." He smiled at me. "You people will make it through, just as we did. Not without cost. I should know all about that, shouldn't I? I paid a high price. The political machine ground me up just as it did him. Do you know what makes it all worthwhile to us early believers? The fact that you people are struggling today. The fact that you tell his story, eat the same bread and wine in his name. The fact that you simply exist and are faithful. That's what makes it all worthwhile to people like me."

He stood up, confident and business-like, very much in charge. As I watched him disappear around the corner of the mosque I had a momentary image of him patiently chairing an endless series of meetings, and doing it very well.